A Simple Way

With our love
Geeco

Geeco Publishing

First Published Amazon Kindle 2022

www.geecopublishing.com

ISBN: 978 1 7391073 4 5

Other books published by Geeco – Enjoy In Joy

Tradition 12

"Anonymity is the spiritual foundation of all our traditions, ever reminding us to place principles before personalities."

This book has been created by the joint efforts of the members of Geeco, and we are equal creators, we offer it to you from our collective name of Geeco.

You can communicate with us at geeco909@gmail.com

If you enjoy the messages in this book, help us to get them out there by leaving a review on Amazon.

Read

Enjoy

Share

Choice

Life offers a cruel choice: you can be right or happy. Not both. This is true regardless of whom you may be involved with, but especially true if there is an emotional vampire in your life.

Albert J. Bernstein

Being right or being happy? Being at peace or being right?

I'd never even considered it. If I had, I'd want both.

Think of something you feel strongly about, feel certain about, and imagine defending your view.

You will feel your body tensing – because you know you're right. You are defending your beliefs.

And, heaven forbid, I'm not saying that your views are wrong (what do I know?). However, the need to be right poisons us. It chews up our peace of mind and spits it out.

Relax. The world won't end if you don't force your views on everyone. They might even like and respect you more.

The issue is you. You are the only thing that truly matters to you. Being at peace, having serenity, ease and joy are far more important than winning.

Let go.

Enjoy your life.

We can never obtain peace in the outer world until we make peace with ourselves.

Dalai Lama

Self-delusion

Of course, that rationalisation didn't work at all. It would have helped if I'd had some Oreo cookie ice cream to eat at the same time. I've learned that self-delusion is much easier when there's something sweet in your mouth.

Lee Goldberg

"Does my bum look big in this?"

"When I brush my hair over, I don't look bald."

"If I don't tuck my shirt in, I won't look as fat as my pregnant wife."

Oh, the insanity of self-delusion. And probably – maybe only possibly – we nearly all have some tiny element of self-delusion, even if it's not as blatant as these.

We almost certainly think we are funny and know more than we do.

And we would feel better about ourselves if we admitted our delusions to ourselves and actually did something about them. Then we might stop worrying about the size of our arse.

There are so many paths to contentment if you're open to self-delusion.

Anthony Marra

The human brain is a complex organ with the wonderful power of enabling man to find reasons for continuing to believe whatever it is that he wants to believe.

Voltaire

Praise

The trouble with most of us is that we would rather be ruined by praise than saved by criticism.

Norman Vincent Peale

We are addicted to praise, to being loved, valued and approved of. Addicted. We crave it, and when we are not getting it, we suffer withdrawals.

From infancy onwards, we were praised and loved when we were good. That is when our addiction started. And so now that is what makes us believe that we don't exist when we are not getting it. We think our identity can only exist when we are being acknowledged.

When we are dependent on others for our wellbeing, they cease to be real to us, and they are just the source of our next fix. We cannot truly love them if we need them for their praise.

We are not experiencing them as real people but as someone who supplies the drug, we crave. Deep within ourselves, if we go there, we can find our being, where we are whole, where we are light. Where we do not need anything to be.

And if we choose to interact with the world from there, our dependency/addiction ceases to exist. We can take our light into the world and share it.

Happiness is within. It has nothing to do with how much applause you get or how many people praise you.
Happiness comes when you believe that you have done something truly meaningful.

Martin Yan

Struggle

The greater the obstacle, the more glory in overcoming it.

Molière

As you start to walk out on the way, the way appears.

Rumi

If you were ever lucky enough to watch a butterfly struggle its way out of its cocoon, you have witnessed the wonder of life, beauty and freedom resulting from its struggle to get out.

If as you watched, you thought, which you might, that the struggle is too great for it, I must help it.

And if you were to help it out?

The chances are that it would come out incomplete. Its wings are not fully exercised, and it might be unable to fly.

Unable to ever fly.

I'm not saying that we cannot assist each other. But for us to reach freedom, we have to make our own way through our struggles.

No one can do it for us.

And having journeyed through them, we will be able to be alive.

You gain strength, courage and confidence by every experience in which you really stop to look fear in the face. You must do the thing you think you cannot do.

Eleanor Roosevelt

January 5

Judgement

Judging a person does not define who they are. It defines who you are.

Wayne Dyer

We can never judge the lives of others because each person knows only their own pain and renunciation. It's one thing to feel that you are on the right path, but it's another to think that yours is the only path.

Paulo Coelho

Years ago, I watched a TV program about long-term residents of mental institutions being released into the community.

They housed a man in a nice enough flat. You could see how thrilled he was to have his freedom. But he didn't keep it tidy. He didn't do his washing up straight away.

So they said, "He isn't coping", and returned him to the locked ward. We are all so different. And so it is very easy to judge, look down on, and think less of others who do not do things the way we do.

Often the differences are very slight. But even little critical thoughts about others are damaging to them and us.

We want to train ourselves to look on and be with others with love and acceptance.

Then the whole world will benefit.

Never judge an eagle by the opinion of turkeys.

Matshona Dhliwayo

The least amount of judging we can do, the better off we are.

Michael J. Fox

Acceptance

*When solving problems, dig at the roots, instead of hacking
at the leaves.*

Anthony J. D'Angelo

All problems are illusions of the mind.

Eckhart Tolle

Usually, when bad things happen in my life, I let go of
them very quickly and move on. I've learnt that dwelling on
them and going over them endlessly only makes me feel bad,
and I don't like that, so I choose not to do it. I may need to
discuss it once with someone. Generally, that is enough.

Occasionally, something happens in my life that is so
huge, devastating, and disturbing that it takes longer. I feel
bad when it is ongoing. Not only about the event itself but
also my inability to discard the negativity it's causing in my
life when I cannot let go quickly.

And then something remarkable happened. I was walking
with a friend, and I put my foot into a large, moist, steaming
pile of dog shit.

(If you are offended by the word shit, I am sorry for you. I
think that calling horse shit horse manure does not change
what it is.)

There it was, clinging excitedly around my immaculate
newish white trainers. I did the wiping on grass, but the
smell travelled on with us when we got back to the car...

Later as I cleaned the remains embedded in the cracks of
the sole, I realised that cleaning it away had to take the time
it took.

And so now, when I'm confronted with significant
turmoil, I accept that it has to run its course before I can let
go of it.

*Most of the problems in life are because of two reasons: we
act without thinking, or we keep thinking without acting.*

Zig Ziglar

January 7

Awareness

Look at everything always as though you were seeing it either for the first time or the last time. Then your time on earth will be filled with glory.

Betty Smith

When I was a kid, my mother would ask me to go and get something for her. (Can't remember what, a book, her watch, her makeup, what it was is unimportant.) I'd go to the room where it was and look and look and look, realise that it was not there, and go and tell her. She would then come to the room with me, show me the thing sitting in full view and say, "There it is!"

This is called a negative hallucination. Our ego, or unconscious, makes the thing invisible to us.

We continue to have negative hallucinations throughout our lives. Not only in terms of things we cannot see but also in behaviours or actions we do not want to process. We are blind to them.

It is worth becoming aware if we are doing this, because the behaviour is in "full view" if we open our mind.

Vision is the art of seeing what is invisible to others.

Jonathan Swift

Love

The greatest gift that you can give to others is the gift of unconditional love and acceptance.

Brian Tracy

Love.

Unconditional love.

Having unconditional love means that we are not making any demands or requests that we will get anything back.

If I allow myself to love someone unconditionally, then I love them, and the truth that comes from that is that I do not expect or need them to love me back, or do anything to prove that they love me.

So if I want them to call me, or be with me, or do things with me, if I want anything so that not having it causes me pain or suffering, then I have stopped loving them unconditionally. I have moved from unconditional love into a state of demand, expectation, hope and longing. I am no longer bathing them with my love. For at some level, I want something in return.

What I do at that moment is up to me. I can choose to suffer, or I can return to unconditional love.

Pain or love?

It should be easy to choose, shouldn't it?

Maybe realising that now will make the choice easier next time.

Love her but leave her wild.

Atticus

Self-awareness

Life is a series of experiences, each one of which makes us bigger, even though sometimes it is hard to realise this. For the world was built to develop character, and we must learn that the setbacks and griefs which we endure help us in our marching onward.

Henry Ford

At the moment I have a hurty toe. That is what the child within me calls it. So I've made an appointment with the hurty toe lady (let's not confuse ourselves with grown-up labels), and she will fix it.

Why do I tell you this?

Because my hurty toe is easy to identify, however, many things in life cause us mental discomfort, and we hardly give them the time of day. We just limp along, suffering them, not considering, not realising how much better off we would be if we acknowledged them and discovered ways to change them so they no longer made us less.

If we puncture ever so slightly a rubber boat, it will go down. Every so often, we pump it up and don't realise it's punctured. But we tend to accumulate a mass of virtually invisible punctures in our lives, and they lessen us.

So acknowledge and identify the things that trouble you and change them. You will benefit, and so will everyone else. Don't die from a thousand pinpricks. You are worth more than that.

If they want peace, nations should avoid the pin-pricks that precede cannon shots.

Napoleon Bonaparte

January 10

Searching

What should I possibly have to tell you, oh venerable one?
Perhaps you're searching far too much? That in all that
searching, you don't find the time for finding?

Hermann Hesse

Many of us are searching for answers, wanting to discover how to be. How to exist. How to change. How to become. How to let go. How to have peace, freedom, and joy. Or maybe even more likely – how to stop suffering.

We read. We search for inspirational teachers, and paths to... enlightenment. No, most of us probably don't believe that is possible, so we don't even look. Just to make living less... unbearable... please... that would do... or it would be a start at any rate.

We, no, you are, in fact, the centre of the universe. Everything that exists in your life, the good, the magnificent and the dreadful, are all there because you are there, creating them.

The way to change anything. Yes, anything, or everything, is to go inside, into the centre, the core of your being and be present in this moment with yourself.

Be there, totally now, and <u>all</u> your troubles and strivings disappear. There is peace. There is oneness.

You are the ruler of your universe. Dare to be. Be present. Have freedom.

No one is ever satisfied where he is... Only the children
know what they're looking for...

Antoine de Saint-Exupéry

I will no longer mutilate and destroy myself in order to find
a secret behind the ruins.

Hermann Hesse

January 11

Texting

*Much unhappiness has come into the world because of
bewilderment and things left unsaid.*

Fyodor Dostoevsky

*I'll eat a bowl of water with a fork before I give a shit about
your opinion of me.*

Fuckology

To text is to lie.
We edit.
We choose our words carefully.
We hide our real feelings.
We invent and distort.
We lie.

If we want to tell the truth about ourselves and possibly make changes in our lives, we want to talk. Face-to-face if possible – though on the phone is better than nothing.

When we are talking, opening and closing our mouth at a reasonable speed, there is a chance that the truth may just manage to bubble out of us.

It will not when we text. When we text, we lie.

If we want to move on in our lives, we want to talk. Otherwise, we will drown.

*Sometimes, reaching out and taking someone's hand is the
beginning of a journey. At other times, it is allowing
another to take yours.*

Vera Nazarian

Compromise

I can accept anything, except what seems to be the easiest for most people: the half-way, the almost, the just-about, the in-between.

Ayn Rand

Never allow someone to be your priority while allowing yourself to be their option.

Mark Twain

Life is a compromise.

How we relate to others, and how we love or tolerate them is a compromise.

To get the best out of life and relationships, we want to take risks. We want to accept the possibility of rejection. For when we don't, we are hiding. We are playing the kid's game of putting our hands over our face and saying, "You can't see me!"

One of our troubles is that everyone, or virtually everyone else, is playing that game too.

If we can find the courage to tell them what is happening inside ourselves, we may make new connections and find new ways to bring joy into the world.

We all know someone who dumps all their troubles on anyone who will listen. I'm not suggesting that you do that.

What I am suggesting is that we start to acknowledge and share our inner being and tell people what they can do, which will make a difference in our lives, rather than allowing them to take us for granted.

Stop making deposits into everyone else's accounts and always leaving yourself overdrawn.

Christine E. Szymanski

Mind

The intuitive mind is a sacred gift and the rational mind is a faithful servant. We have created a society that honours the servant and has forgotten the gift.

Albert Einstein

What a waste. What a shame. Though not when you think about it, a surprise. After all, our ego creates this world and does all it can to control us. It does not want us to get in touch with and be guided by our inner voice.

The inner voice is where intuition and oneness with god exists.

We can, of course, go to our inner voice, our inner god, whenever we want to. We just have to remember and choose to do it.

We can be a light in the world.

Be the light and source of inspiration that others see.

Sunday Adelaja

We can be the light of the world without leaving our high beams on and annoying everybody.

Bob Goff

Thoughts

Instead of worrying about what you cannot control, shift your energy to what you can create.

Roy T. Bennett

Every thought we have creates. The more often we have it, the stronger the creation.

Every time we expect, say, or idly imagine anything bad or negative in our lives, it is more likely to become a reality.

Likewise, every positive thought or expectation becomes a reality.

Which would you prefer?

What are you thinking, expecting, hoping for, and dreaming about?

Is now the moment to decide how you will orchestrate everything?

A blank piece of paper is God's way of telling us how hard it is to be God.

Sidney Sheldon

First things first, but not necessarily in that order.

Dr Who

Self-doubt

*I seek strength, not to be greater than others, but to fight
my greatest enemy, the doubts within myself.*

P. C. Cast

People pay us compliments.

And even if they don't, they say things about us that we
hear. Others inform us, at some level, what they think about
us by their reaction to us.

We are constantly bombarded with feedback about the
sort of person we are.

So, what do we do with this information?

Even the expectational people amongst us, those who
seem to be in control of their lives and the world, suffer from
self-doubt. While they accept most of the compliments with
ease, there is still that little voice which asks them, "Are they
serious? Are they saying that as a put-down, not a
compliment?"

And if they, the wonderful, the beautiful ones, think that,
then what hope is there for ordinary mortals like you and
me?

Although if they doubt themselves, it is understandable
that we would too.

Thinking about it, if we realise that their self-doubt is
wrong, it's just their ego sticking the knife in, then that is
also true of our self-doubt.

We are more okay than we think.

In fact, we are okay. So let us rejoice and enjoy our lives.

*I don't believe anyone ever suspects how completely unsure
I am of my work and myself and what tortures of self-
doubting the doubt of others has always given me.*

Tennessee Williams

January 16

Self-defence

In silence and in self-defence, I figured things out in my own little way.

Loretta Young

When we are threatened physically, we defend ourselves. (Even if our defence is to curl up into a ball whilst the blows reign down on us.)

And yet we allow mental attacks to batter, belittle and poison us without a thought.

How can we allow the damaging and negative that flood over us from the news or social media without defending ourselves?

Even the simple online "Look at me, I'm so wonderful and perfect" bullshit that we digest when we stare at the lives of others attacks our being at the core.

For your peace of mind and your health, stop absorbing that poison.

A tree never hits an automobile except in self-defence.

Woody Allen

January 17

Happiness

No medicine cures what happiness cannot.

Gabriel García Marquez

What would make you happy?

That is not a frivolous question.

And it is one that so many of us have never considered asking ourselves.

We might have thought I would be happy if I had that toy, girlfriend or boyfriend, house, job or game. But nearly all of them are, at best, just a distraction from our unhappiness.

So, what would make you happy?

Dig deep.

Dig deeper.

Find your answer. Spend time there every day.

Your ego will claw you away from it. Learn to discard the ego and return to what makes you happy.

How simple it is to see that we can only be happy now, and there will never be a time when it is not now.

Gerald Jampolsky

Ego

I have never seen a greater monster or miracle than myself.

Michel de Montaigne

Ego Trip: a journey to nowhere.

Robert Half

Many of us were encouraged to develop a strong Ego when we were young. To be assertive, take charge of our lives and lead others to do what we wanted or needed them to do. We were told that if we failed to do this, people would take advantage of us, and we would fail.

Whilst there may be an element of truth in that, our ego is, in fact, at war with the world and with ourselves. It creates the world it wants, and it does not care if others suffer to achieve this. Nor does it care if we suffer.

It likes us to suffer, just enough to have self-doubt and negative emotions.

When we mention the ego in this book, we are always talking about the destructive ego. The unhelpful, self-critical voice that is constantly finding ways to make you doubt yourself. It does not want you to succeed or to be happy. We suggest ways to find harmony within yourself, away from the ravages of the ego.

Our ego is our silent partner – too often with a controlling interest.

Cullen Hightower

Yeah But

Everything… affects everything.

Jay Asher

Let no man pull you so low as to hate him.

Martin Luther King

"But", and his even more offensive mate, "Yeah But!"

When someone says "Yeah But" to us, it means "I haven't been listening to anything you've been saying (because I know it's all rubbish) – so listen to what I have to say. This is the truth! This is what matters, and quite frankly, I don't respect you anyway!"

So there, now you know. And what is our only possible, mature response to being "Yeah, But-ted?"

We hold up our hand. We say, "Stop. If all you can do is disrespect me with a Yeah But, go and talk to someone else."

We can explain the first time why being "Yeah But-ted" is so offensive. And from then on, we want to terminate the conversation. If you are on the phone, hang up.

"But surely", you cry, "isn't that taking it a bit too far?" Well, I don't think so. I don't believe that people who disrespect us that much deserve our company.

They will either learn or move on from us. And if they refuse to learn, then why do we want them in our life?

Poisonous relationships cloud your vision. I wasted a lot of time adjusting my personal boundaries and justifying disrespect when it would have been so much easier (and a lot less painful) to simply adjust my life to their absence.

Steve Maraboli

Love

Being deeply loved by someone gives you strength, while loving someone deeply gives you courage.

Lao Tzu

She said to me, "If I die, don't miss me. Just be grateful that we had this time together."

She did. And I did miss her. I do miss her. But...

But I am so incredibly grateful that we had our time together. What a miracle that was.

What a miracle it is that we meet and spend time with anyone. We want to relish our life.

So often, we just take things and people for granted.

It takes an effort to engage with others. If we do not want to engage with them, we want to question whether we should be with them.

We are only here once (this time around), and we want to enjoy it.

When I discover who I am, I'll be free.

Ralph Ellison

Men love women, women love children, children love hamsters, hamsters don't love anybody.

Alice Thomas Ellis

Lying

The man who lies to himself and listens to his own lie comes to such a pass that he cannot distinguish the truth within him.

Fyodor Dostoevsky

People ask us how we are, and we lie.
"Well, I don't."

Honestly? We edit. We make things better or worse. We highlight or hide things for effect.

We listen to ourselves, and we often even fool ourselves. Buying into the fabrications, we weave.

Yes, we do occasionally tell the truth, but often it is so overwhelming by then that we cannot absorb it.

It is so important to have one person with whom we can be honest. Totally honest.

If you do not have one, go and experiment with some of the people you know, being more and more honest until you find the person you can honestly talk to.

It will make a significant difference in your life.

A wonderful gift may not be wrapped as you expect.

Jonathan Lockwood Huie

Secrets

If we knew each other's secrets, what comforts we should find.

John Churton Collins

If you eat 12 doughnuts a day, and everyone knows you do, it is okayish, but it may not be a good idea.

If you eat 12 doughnuts a day and pretend that you don't, that is not okay.

(Please feel free to substitute the words doughnuts and eat.)

The moment we deny or keep a secret, we are lying. We are lying to the world and ourselves. We are on a sledge going down a hill with no brakes. God alone knows how long the hill is or what's at the bottom, and he ain't telling.

It is so important that we do not have secrets. I'm not saying that everyone must know our innermost thoughts or deeds. But we want to have one person, to tell the truth to.

As long as we have a person we are talking to, one day, we may be happy within ourselves.

If we are on our own, then the twelve doughnuts will slowly and inevitably increase.

(This writing may appear to be about addiction, but it isn't, it's about everything in our lives.)

Nothing makes us so lonely as our secrets.

Paul Tournier

Freedom

Now, we're just here to be memories for our kids.

Jonathan & Christopher Nolan

Don't stop living.

Don't stop getting out there and doing things.

Don't be the person that tells their kids "No" all the time—trying (and I use that word deliberately) trying to control them. As Kahlil Gibran says, "You are the bows from which your children as living arrows are sent forth," so do not try to control them.

Instead, be an example of excellence. I realise that most people have no concept of what that might be. But I am sure that you are different.

Leave aside all the failures and dreadful mistakes of the past. They're fine. There's nothing you can do about them now. Sorry about that.

Now demonstrate love with all the excellence you can muster. Lead by example rather than with criticism. Get them involved in their life and living. Help them experience the joys of doing things for and with others.

Give them freedom.

And give yourself freedom too. Go out and live. Go out and do. Don't let them remember you stuck in front of your TV.

Go out.

Enjoy.

Freedom is not worth having if it does not include the freedom to make mistakes.

Mahatma Gandhi

The only real prison is fear, and the only real freedom is freedom from fear.

Aung San Suu Kyi

January 24

Choice

There is a time in every life when paths are chosen,
character is forged. I could have chosen a different path,
but I didn't. I failed myself.

Libba Bray

Oh my God, what a dreadful confession. And she dares to think or speak about it.

So many of us won't even acknowledge that things could or should be different. And so we gasp our way through our lives, unfulfilled. A trembling shadow, a ghost of the person we could be.

Yes, if we were to dare to make changes – even little ones – we would be faced with difficulties, challenges and almost certainly pain. Maybe even vast pain.

But the payoff!? To be free, able to walk with our head held high, our shoulders back, and our face creased with a smile.

And it is not impossible. We can change.

Or we can choose to continue to live our life in the half-light, in some kind of a lie.

I don't know your circumstances. All I can do is toss a pebble into a lake. Whether you choose to notice the ripples or not is up to you.

I only wish you deep joy.

You can't cross the sea merely by standing and staring at
the water.

Rabindranath Tagore

When you make a choice, you change the future.

Deepak Chopra

Choose well. Your choice is brief, and yet endless.

Goethe

Trust

You may be deceived if you trust too much, but you will live in torment if you don't trust enough.

Frank Crane

Let's talk about God.

(I know it's a subject we should never discuss, but ...)

Some people know, absolutely, without a shadow of a doubt, everything about their God, which is wonderful for them.

Some people have absolutely no idea who or what God is or might be, but they still believe that there is some more significant power than us.

Some believe in universal energy, while others believe there is no God.

Leaving aside the ones who know there is no God, most of us find ourselves praying, even if only at extreme times.

And many of us do trust in God. But do we honestly have the faith to let go?

What is the difference between trust and faith?

You are watching a circus act, and a man is being pushed along a high wire in a wheelbarrow without a safety net. As you watch, you trust that they will not fall.

Faith is when you are the man in the wheelbarrow.

If you have faith that God is present in your life, it makes your journey easier.

None of us knows what might happen even in the next minute, yet still we go forward. Because we trust. Because we have faith.

Paulo Coelho

Behaviour

*Most people are asleep and need to be confronted, like
adults that are still behaving like they're 5 years old, and
don't want to assume responsibility for their mistakes.*

Robin Sacredfire

Do you remember what you were like as a child? Take a
little while to think back and work out what you did to get
your way.

Did you rage or sulk? Were you open or sneaky? Did you
share things, or did you keep them a secret? Were you mean
or generous? Were you considerate, or did you push your
way to the front? Did you do anything to ensure that you
won, or were you not too bothered about winning? You just
wanted to enjoy the game.

Did you laugh at other people's misfortunes and make
fun of them, or were you supportive? Were you able to laugh
at things when they went wrong for you, or did anger and
retaliation spread through you like an out-of-control flame?
Were you honest about how much money you had, or did
you want to keep it a secret?

Did you do your best to control the situation and others,
or were you easygoing? Were you always under someone
else's control, waiting to be told what to do, unable to make
decisions alone? Did you generally feel right or wrong?

Do you think the ways you behaved then were right?
Almost certainly, some decisions you made then were often
not the right choices.

The chances are that most of your current behaviours are
the same as those you had as a child. Do you think it's time
to make some changes?

*When one came to know them, it was surprising how
childish grown people can be.*

Rumer Godden

Daffodils

And then my heart with pleasure fills
And dances with the daffodils.

William Wordsworth

I am enveloped in the scent of daffodils.
(And one doesn't normally connect daffodils with scent.)
I am sitting with the golden light crying out to me. Shouting out, "There is hope!" "Life goes on!" "Sunlight will return!"
I am sitting bathed in joy.
The days are getting longer.
I am getting younger.
I want to dance. To hold my daffodils aloft and shout out to passers-by, "Look! Look! Look!" "Spring is coming!" "I am alive!"

She turned to the sunlight
And shook her yellow head
And whispered to her neighbour:
"Winter is dead".

A. A. Milne

Arguments

You can't win an argument. You can't because if you lose it, you lose it, and if you win it, you lose it.

Dale Carnegie

When was the last time you lost an argument? Did you do it through clenched teeth? And carry your disappointment, if that's what you call it, around with you for ages?

Just questions. Things to ponder. How do you feel when confronted? Do you pull on your battle gear immediately? Of course, perhaps you concede without a fight before doing everything you are told to do. If that is the case, you probably live in the wrong place and with the wrong people. Changing that is almost certainly a good idea.

If you cling to your arguments, you will discover new freedom and a new pleasure by walking away from them. Take a deep breath and let go of them. It's not worth fighting your corner all the time, and it consumes our energy, our well-being, and our ability to have peace. We are more valuable to ourselves than an argument.

Live.

Enjoy.

It's hard to win an argument with a smart person, but it's damn near impossible to win an argument with a stupid person.

Bill Murray

Deciding

Success is doing what you want to do, when you want, where you want, with whom you want, as much as you want.

Tony Robbins

I only ever do what I want to do. You probably think how unbelievably selfish. How can anyone do that? That can't be true.

For a vast amount of my life, in my ignorance, I virtually only did what I had to do, what I should do. I did things because I believed I had no choice. I was not happy. (Not being happy is a very mild expression of how I felt.)

Then, one day, I changed.

I changed completely. It didn't happen overnight. I have no idea how long the change took. It may have taken weeks or even years. I do not know. But I have changed.

I decided I would no longer do anything I didn't want to do. I don't have to wash up, and I don't have to go to work if I don't want to. But, I can and I do decide that I want to do these things, so I do them with pleasure because I am doing what I want to do.

Sometimes something gets left undone for ages (or even forever), but the world hasn't ended because of that, so I guess it can wait.

Start doing what you want to do, and everything else will be revealed to you.

Paulo Coelho

Gold

*There is a sun, a light that for want of another word I can
only call yellow, pale sulphur yellow, pale golden citron.
How lovely yellow is!*

Vincent Van Gogh

Let us have a golden moment together. That sounds
pretty wonderful, doesn't it?

Breathing slowly, with a slight smile, go inside, into your
being.

Find that spark of rich golden light, the warm pulsating
goldenness, and smile with it.

Let it grow, spreading through your body.

Now holding you completely, its warmth gently sparkling
throughout you.

Let it spread out, becoming ever more golden as it
envelopes everyone nearby.

As it so spreads, pulling your whole neighbourhood into
its golden smile. And now encompassing your city, your
country and expanding its radiance and smile growing as it
hugs the world and everything and everybody in and on the
planet.

Golden smiling love.

*In meditation, when your mind becomes perfectly still and
calm, you will experience the golden light of eternity.*

Frederick Lindemann

Hell

I think Hell is something you carry around with you. Not somewhere you go.

Neil Gaiman

If you have never experienced hell on earth, or you are not there right now, then it is hard to imagine or process.

But it exists.

There was a time when I was there. Totally. I thought that whatever came after this had to be better. I believed that God was just playing a horrible joke on us. Thankfully with the help of AA and a God of my understanding, I am now at peace, happy, and serene (most of the time).

The God, of my understanding, is not the institutionalised God. I have friends who go to church, which is wonderful for them. When I go to a church service, I feel God's presence. But I don't particularly appreciate being told what I should believe or how to behave, so I cannot buy into any conventional view. I do my best to live a good, generous, and non-critical life. I do my best not to look down on others just because I don't like their views.

Doing my best means that I do not always succeed, but I succeed more often than not. I feel centred and blessed.

Trauma is hell on earth. Trauma resolved is a gift from the Gods.

Peter A. Levine

It is easy to go down into Hell, night and day, the gates of dark Death stand wide, but to climb back again, to retrace one's steps to the upper air – there's the rub, the task.

Virgil

Enjoy

February 1

Waking

Every time you come in yelling that God damn "Rise and shine!" "Rise and shine!" I say to myself, "How lucky dead people are!"

Tennessee Williams

When you wake and move towards rising, do you think, "I don't want to get up?" or do you leap from your bed with enthusiasm, joy, and excitement?

Perhaps enthusiasm is too much to expect, maybe to have pleasure as you view your day ahead is enough.

But the "I don't want to get up" is something that deserves our investigation. What is it about our life that makes us want to hide from it? Why do we want to pull the covers over our head and disappear?

There must be things going on that we do not want any longer. And unless we look at them and identify them, they will almost certainly worsen.

We need to talk them over honestly with someone else to find a way through. We want to dare to say things we have perhaps refused to acknowledge.

We'll have to work out where we go from there when we know what the challenge is. Even if we decide to continue to live with it for the moment, knowing the cause will enable us to cope more easily.

Of course, if we wish, we can just go on not wanting to get up, but that would be sad, surely.

I arise in the morning torn between a desire to improve the world and a desire to enjoy the world.

E. B. White

Intention

A garden requires patient labour and attention. Plants do not grow merely to satisfy ambitions or to fulfil good intentions. They thrive because someone expended effort on them.

Liberty Hyde Bailey

What is your intention?

What is your intention for today, and what is it that draws you further into your life?

So many of us just stumble through our day without thought, without direction, reacting to the immediate situation like an invisible speck of dust, blown here and then there.

If we have an intention for today, something to achieve, some way to be, some behaviour to focus on, our day will be richer, more fulfilling, and we will achieve more.

If we also have a long-term intention, we will find that our life is guided and so much more whole than when we just drift along.

It is a good idea to spend a few moments at some regular time in the morning to consider our day and pick something we intend to do or some behaviour we will focus on for the day. And also look ahead at the direction we choose to take our lives.

Of course, just reading this, and moving on without thought, will change nothing.

Choose self-empowerment.

If you haven't found it yet, keep looking.

Steve Jobs

Parents

Parents are the bones on which children cut their teeth.

Peter Ustinov

So much is asked of parents, and so little is given.

Virginia Satir

Parents are strange people.

It's not their fault.

Most of them don't know any better.

They just teach what they learnt as kids, or they teach the opposite.

And what they learnt goes back many generations.

Although kids are strange people too, even when they're grown up.

So, I guess... that must make us... strange.

We have our parent's behaviours and beliefs battling within us, filling us with feelings of inadequacy and guilt, or anger and rebellion.

It is rare to be able to change our relationship with them from one of parent/child to one of friendship and equality.

Our mother doesn't even have to say anything, she just comes in and looks at our room or us or listens to what we have to say, and we know we've failed again.

Perhaps if we were to dare to challenge or question their behaviours, it might change, and if it does, it is worth it.

It is doubly worth doing if we are parents ourselves. Don't pass your great-grandparent's tunnel vision beliefs onto your children. They don't deserve it.

Children begin by loving their parents, as they grow older they judge them, sometimes they forgive them.

Oscar Wilde

Remembering

We do not remember days, we remember moments.

Cesare Pavese

Bad times, moments, and experiences happen to us. Sometimes they are ghastly, suicidal blackness totally enveloping us. Then, in the same way that we forget physical pain, we forget how awful it was, and we move on. It is our way of protecting ourselves. And thank God that we do that, rather than constantly carrying the horror of it.

However, as we begin to pick our way out of the mental disaster, we can, in some way, bookmark that moment in our minds. Then the next time things start to go badly, we can remember the end of the pain rather than the event itself.

Whatever we are going through will pass. Everything that we have ever felt or experienced has passed. We know that. Do not let the present difficulty lie to you that it is endless.

Discard the pain. Bookmark its demise.

Take a few minutes now, go back to the end of some awfulness and bookmark your departure from it.

Remember to breathe. It is, after all, the secret of life.

Gregory Maguire

My fake plants died because I did not pretend to water them.

Mitch Hedberg

February 5

Freedom

I have learnt that by suppressing the dark aspects of myself, I was not loving me, the whole me. As I embrace these aspects, these rejected aspects and integrate the shadows into my light, I am learning to love all of me. The whole me.

Angela Hughes

Oh, the dark and hidden sides of ourselves, so often ignored as they crouch in the shadows. Just waiting and waiting quietly. Patiently. So very patient. Some we may have even (apparently) completely forgotten about.

And the truth is that if we do our soul searching alone, uncover defects, and then simply re-cover them, nothing will have changed.

To embrace and love ourselves, we have to share our secrets, our hidden aspects, with someone else. Telling them disempowers the secrets.

We can then be free.

We can then love ourselves.

Our whole selves.

The secret to happiness is freedom, and the secret to freedom is courage.

Thucydides

Freedom means the opportunity to be what we never thought we would be.

Daniel J. Boorstin

Put-Downs

Are you in great physical pain, or is that your thinking expression?

G. A. Aiken

If your brains were dynamite, there wouldn't be enough to blow your hat off.

Kurt Vonnegut

Put-downs. Jokes at our expense.

Other people's unsaid expectation that we will not succeed.

They all pull the plug on us, and we swirl away into the vortex of failure.

They do not even need to be very bad for us to doubt and question ourselves, to feel that we have to prove, again and again, that we are okay.

To change this, to not have to be drained, we want to start questioning them and challenging the things they are saying or implying.

"Do you want me to fail?"

"Are you saying that, so I won't succeed?"

"Are you trying to belittle me?"

"Am I just a laughingstock?"

When we ask these or similar questions, they will take stock of what they're saying. So often, people say bad things out of habit or because they think it's funny. But when we challenge them (two or three times if necessary), they will stop.

If they don't stop or they say they want you to fail, then you no longer want to be around them.

All morons hate it when you call them a moron.

J. D. Salinger

Self-doubt

*What problems do you have, apart from being blind,
unemployed and a moron?*

John McEnroe

Put-downs. Jokes at our expense.

(No, it's not being repeated by mistake.)

This time, we are the culprit. We belittle and doubt ourselves. And we are very good at it.

So, this time, when we say to ourselves, "You can't do that." "You're going to fail." "Again!"

We want to say to our ego, 'No. I'm not interested in that. I'm not going to think about that anymore. I'm going to succeed.'

Your ego wants you to fail. As long as you are failing, it is in control.

When you refuse to listen to it, when you shut it down, it will keep trying to make you doubt yourself.

But persist.

Keep rebuffing it.

Refuse to listen to it.

It will weaken.

It will quieten down.

It will, of course, be looking for new and different ways to damage you. So, you will want to deal with them as they arise.

The alternative to our ego and fear is our higher self. And when we go into our hearts for the answers, the ego is shut down.

*The man who moves a mountain begins by carrying away
small stones.*

Confucius

February 8

Interaction

In a closed society where everybody's guilty, the only crime is getting caught. In a world of thieves, the only final sin is stupidity.

Hunter S. Thompson

You are living with a thief.

It is consuming your life, raping your mind, sucking freedom from your soul.

Your phone is not your friend.

"Oh, come on! It is! It is vital! It gives me everything I need!"

But at what cost?

Social media, emails and texts, games, or research consume your mind, making it dart from this to the next mental interruption.

I am not guiltless. I am weak too. I am sometimes lured into believing that it helps me.

But how can I be genuinely living when I allow it to interrupt what I am doing with its call or vibration?

If you and I sat and chatted and I spent the whole time looking over your shoulder and around the room, would you feel I was treating you with the respect you deserve?

Suppose I go into a garden filled with natural beauty and spend my time looking at a screen. Well? Why have a garden?

I only mention any of this because I hope it makes me think. That it helps me to challenge the way I behave.

The present moment is filled with joy and happiness. If you are attentive, you will see it.

Thich Nhat Hanh

Responsibility

Accept responsibility for your life. Know that it is you who will get you where you want to go, no one else.

Les Brown

You must take personal responsibility. You cannot change the circumstances, the seasons, or the wind, but you can change yourself. That is something you have charge of.

Jim Rohn

It's not all about you.

We so easily and often drag everything back to us, how it makes us feel. How "they" don't do the "right" thing. How "they" always do the "wrong" thing.

Okay, so maybe <u>you</u> want to tone that down. Perhaps, things don't go quite how you'd like them to, and your good feelings diminish.

It is essential to remember that "they" can't make you feel anything. They can't make you feel insecure, sad, abandoned, isolated, angry, unloved, pathetic, or resentful. They can't do that to you. You do it to yourself. You turn on the unhappiness tap and bathe in it.

You are either part of the problem or part of the solution in any situation. If you are going to talk to others about what is going on, you want to look at your involvement in the situation and become aware of how you are part of the problem.

When you've looked at your part in its cause, you can become open to moving into becoming part of the solution. Then you can discuss it with others. If you simply go to them with just the problem, you might as well go into their house and smash it up.

When you think everything else is someone else's fault, you will suffer a lot. When you realise that everything springs only from yourself, you will learn both peace and joy.

Dalai Lama

Involvement

The only real mistake is the one from which we learn nothing.

Henry Ford

Things happen.

People die, and there are accidents and disasters. And when we are involved in any of them, we take them personally.

But things happen in the world all the time. So, if (and it may be a big if) we can accept what appears to be happening to us as just "things happening", we can change how we process them.

If we do that, we can distance ourselves from them and not dive into all the negativity we create in our lives, bodies, and souls when we claim involvement or responsibility.

If you spin a coin and call heads and it comes down tails, that is not something that has happened to you or that you are responsible for. It is just a thing happening.

Learn to let go of things. Better still, discover how not to pick them up in the first place.

You're here. Enjoy.

The difference between involvement and commitment is like ham and eggs. The chicken is involved; the pig is committed.

Martina Navratilova

Moving on

Someone I loved once gave me a box full of darkness. It took me years to understand that this too, was a gift.

Mary Oliver

Life has its ups and downs. The good and the bad. And a great many of us have had some incredibly black moments.

Times when we have felt incapable of any action, consumed with fear and dread. We may even have looked for a way out: drugs, alcohol, suicide. The way ahead felt totally impossible.

The chances are that reading this now, you think to yourself, "Well, it was never that bad." But even if it was "that bad" at the time, the chances are that you cannot recall its awfulness now.

We move on from the event and the agony. Our unconscious changes and lessens the pain as time passes because to continue to feel with that intensity would be unbearable.

Why do I mention any of this? Because what we are struggling through today, or maybe challenged by in the future, will change. It will pass. We will arrive beyond it, and the difficulties and pain it creates in us will diminish.

And so, if we were clever enough to remember this, as some event or situation leaps from the floor and sinks its teeth into our leg, we could lessen its bite by knowing it will pass.

A day, a week, a year from now, it will no longer gnaw at our soul and peace of mind.

I could tell you my adventures – beginning from this morning, but it's no use going back to yesterday, because I was a different person then.

Lewis Carroll

Nature

*Look deep into nature, and then you will understand
everything better.*

Albert Einstein

Nature.

How little most of us bother to engage with it.

Yes, we may take a moment now and then to notice and
think, or even say how lovely, how beautiful, but then we
scoot back into all the important things in our lives.

To benefit, to profit at a spiritual level, we want to go into
it and stop.

Stop everything. Feel the ground beneath us, connect
ourselves to the earth. Listen. Really listen. What do you
hear? Go into, become part of the sounds. Look. Look at
what's around you on the ground and in the air. Absorb it.
Touch the things growing, or the earth, hug a tree, smell
leaves, flowers, anything, everything. Open your soul and
connect with it all. Breathe deeply and slowly. Smile. Become
one with all that is around you.

Repeat often.

Improve your quality of life.

*A monk asks: "Is there anything more miraculous than the
wonders of nature?" The master answers: "Yes, your
awareness of the wonders of nature."*

Angelus Silesius

The sky is the daily bread of the eyes.

Ralph Waldo Emerson

Work

The most common way people give up their power is by thinking they don't have any.

Alice Walker

Why are you in that job?

Why are you doing what you do most days, most of the time?

For some of you, it's an all-consuming obsession or love affair, which is truly wonderful.

Some of you decided as children or teenagers what you would do or be. And so here you are, twenty or forty years later, still doing it.

But is it fulfilling? Would you go to a child or a teenager for career advice?

Most of us just fell into what we do with a haphazard series of events. For instance, it's what your parents did or what was available when you started to look for a job.

So, I ask again, "Why are you in that job?"

If they are honest, most people are in their job because of fear. Fear of being without it.

And yet many people do change careers and find happiness doing what they enjoy and what inspires them. And so, I ask for a third time, "Why are you in that job?"

If other people can change, then why not you too? Don't you deserve to be doing something you like to do? And if none of this applies to you, perhaps you know someone to whom you could ask the question.

The future depends on what you do today.

Mahatma Gandhi

Relationships

Failed relationships can be described as so much wasted make-up.

Marian Keyes

You can victimise yourself by wallowing around in your own past.

Wayne Dyer

Why are you in that relationship?

This isn't necessarily just to do with the people you live with. It might be to do with your parents, work colleagues, relatives, or friends.

I ask the question because so often we go on seeing people, doing things with them, because we always have, although we no longer enjoy it. If that is the case, then ask yourself the question, because doing things with people whose company we do not like is a massive negative drain. If our hearts don't leap with joy when they call us, then we want to question whether to continue to see them or not.

And then we come to partners. Is there oneness and respect in your relationship? Do you both do things for each other with pleasure? Or are you just dragging along because of fear? Or because of the children – which is a lousy reason. When we are not happy, we create unhappiness and insecurity in those around us, even more so in our children, who pick up and absorb any distress we feel.

Yes, ending any relationship is complex. Maybe the consequences will make our lives difficult for a while. But in the end, when we've made our way through the challenges, we will be better off because we will have self-respect.

Think about any attachments that are depleting your emotional reserves. Consider letting them go.

Oprah Winfrey

February 15

Enabling

Our lives begin to end the day we become silent about things that matter.

Martin Luther King

We enable people, the people in our lives, to behave the way they do.

We allow them to behave how they want and to treat us as we have taught them to do.

We do this at home and work. With our children, our parents, and our partners.

And nearly all of us are taken advantage of in some way or another.

Some people simply do not contribute to the world they live in. They plonk themselves down and are waited upon. If we are unfortunate enough to encounter one, we are very unlucky. However, we are enabling them. We are making their behaviour possible.

The saddest thing is that most people are unaware of this. They just think that that's how it is, and they can do nothing about it.

I would like to suggest that there are things that you can do. You do not have to put up with their behaviour. You can refuse to accept it anymore.

Not easy, but not impossible.

Make a stand. Make changes. Stop being a slave.

For what it's worth: it's never too late to be whoever you want to be. I hope you live a life you're proud of, and if you find that you're not, I hope you have the strength to start over.

F. Scott Fitzgerald

Loss

*Anyone who thinks fallen leaves are dead has never
watched them dancing on a windy day.*

Shira Tamir

One leaf has clung to the tree outside my window for
what seems like forever but can only be a few months.

I've spent hours (probably) watching as it has fluttered
and hung on.

"Good morning," I've greeted it, "what's it like out there
today?"

And "Hello, old friend. Well windy last night, eh!"

And other such secret messages of love.

And today, it was gone.

"NO!!"

I dashed outside in the hope I might find it. I searched
and searched.

But no.

So now, I will continue to discuss the beauty of the sky
and the joy of spring. I shall look at our time together with
pleasure. Not with sorrow. Memories want to be joyful.
Places we can go and smile and be with the ones we love.

This is a foreign notion for many, as they rekindle the
pain of their loss. But those we love want us to be happy. We
want to choose happy memories and delight in them.

*It takes one thought, one second, one moment or positive
memory to act as a catalogue for the light to gradually seep
in again.*

Fearne Cotton

February 17

Acceptance

A man cannot be comfortable without his own approval.

Mark Twain

You are on track.

You are in the right place, interacting with the right people, for both of your journeys.

I know, at times, that feels impossible. How or why on earth would you be going through what is happening to you now?

And you, we, fight against it. Doing everything in our power to change it. And that's fine. Perhaps that's where the path leads.

But understanding, knowing that you are in the right place, whether you like it or not, changes your experience.

Understanding that you are in the right place removes much of the struggle. It becomes easier to go through.

Happiness can only exist in acceptance.

George Orwell

It's best to accept life as it really is and not as I imagined it to be.

Paulo Coelho

Suffering

*Walk together. Feel the heartbeats. Experience the presence.
This is how to be thankful.*

Amit Ray

*Pain insists upon being attended to. God whispers to us in
our pleasures, speaks in our conscience, but shouts in our
pains. It is His megaphone to rouse a deaf world.*

C. S. Lewis

When we suffer, when we are filled with pain, fear, and
are totally enveloped, with no way out, and even when it is
far less violent, we feel trapped. None of our solutions hold
any hope. And we can so easily spiral down even further.

If, as you read the above, you are not suffering, or your
troubles seem slight by comparison, there probably have
been times when you were in blackness.

If now (or in the future) you are suffering, the best way to
change it is to stop, go into the pain, in your body and mind,
and say, "Thank you."

Doing this starts the process of disarming it. It opens the
door to its end.

"But I can't. I won't thank it! Do you think I'm mad?"

I understand your cry. [Been there, done that.]

However, all the growth you've made in your life, all the
things that have created the fantastic person you are, have
come about because of the challenges you have gone
through.

So change the pain you have by thanking it. Do it again.
And again. And you will feel it beginning to dissolve, and you
will be able to change the causes. You will begin to be able to
live again.

*One word, frees us of all the weight and pain of life: that
word is love.*

Sophocles

Laughter

If you find it hard to laugh at yourself, I would be happy to do it for you.

Groucho Marx

You've got to laugh. At life, that is. If you didn't, it would be unbearable. Perhaps that's all that is wrong with the world? It's stopped laughing. It takes everything so seriously.

We had a water incident in our kitchen yesterday. Massive, over the soles of our shoes. I won't bore you with the details of its arrival.

So there I was, mop and bucket, mop wringing in it. Enthusiastically mopping and wringing, wringing and mopping, you get the picture. And my wife comes in to help? And she says, "Look, there is a big hole in the bucket."

You've got to laugh. Life is too short to be taken seriously.

If you can laugh at yourself, you're going to be fine, if you allow others to laugh with you, you will be great.

Martin Niemoller

Compassion

If you want others to be happy, practice compassion. If you want to be happy, practice compassion.

Dalai Lama

I'm sure you know that.

Sympathy is observing and accepting what someone is going through. It is detached.

Empathy is when we mentally go into the situation and experience what they are feeling ourselves.

Compassion involves not only feeling the other person's pain, but doing something about it. Helping.

Helping.

Love and compassion are necessities, not luxuries. Without them, humanity cannot survive.

Dalai Lama

Opposites

*The attitude of faith is the very opposite of clinging to belief,
of holding on.*

Alan Watts

There are opposites to everything. We have to have tall
for there to be short. Thin to entertain fat. Dark to know
light.

There is a temptation amongst humans to focus on what
is happening to us at this moment and forget that it has an
opposite.

We notice something bad in our lives and dive deeper and
deeper into the pain and turmoil it can create for us.

And even when we remember this, the effort required to
change our point of view is frequently too great. So much
easier to focus on the negative.

No, we do not do that all the time. In fact, if we are lucky,
we may find it difficult to remember the last mega-neg we
bathed in. But our little displeasures at the world are so
easily grasped by us.

Close your eyes for a moment and become aware of the
darkness. All you need to do is open them to let in the light.

If we change our focus, everything changes.

If we want to have better experiences most of the time,
then that is what we can choose.

Very easy. Really. If we choose.

*The opposite of love is not hate, it's indifference. The
opposite of art is not ugliness, it's indifference. The opposite
of faith is not heresy, it's indifference. The opposite of life is
not death, it's indifference.*

Elie Wiesel

Judgement

If you judge people, you have no time to love them.

Mother Teresa

We all have moments of feeling "less than" others. We also have times when we feel "more than" others. And both feelings damage us. Both forms of judgement chip away at our inner being.

Someone said that the only normal people are the ones we don't know. And interestingly, most people look down on normal people. Even if we may secretly want what they have, we despise them.

It is a dilemma. And one that we have been locked into, to a certain extent, all our lives.

Of course, comparing ourselves, warts and all, to their brilliance on social media or their apparent ease in social or business situations does not make our lives any easier.

One of our problems is that we have gotten used to taking a tablet to relieve our mental and physical pains. We have grown accustomed to expecting the easy way out.

However, we can change. We can stop looking endlessly at social media etc., though we probably won't, too much effort.

But by recognising that the images others present of themselves are lies, it is easier to ignore the rubbish in our heads.

Just because they annoy you doesn't mean they're wrong.

Auliq Ice

Letting go

Life is a series of natural and spontaneous changes. Don't resist them; that only creates sorrow. Let reality be reality. Let things flow naturally forward in whatever way they like.

Lao Tzu

Fear is the mind-killer.

Frank Herbert

Serenity. We have a choice.

So often, we don't believe we have a choice. We feel like the pail of water bouncing down the hill in front of Jack and Jill.

I was the pail of water, convinced that there was nothing I could do. And yet...

I learnt that as long as I <u>tried</u> to be in control of people, places and things, the less I could move forward.

While sometimes I achieved a lot, I never honestly felt I had any control. I suspected that sooner or later, everything would tumble down. Of course, I could not admit that to myself or (obviously) to anyone else.

Then one day, I surrendered. I let go of it all. I handed it over to something greater than myself – what some people call God, the Universe, the light within. I handed it over and said, "Okay, you're in charge – I'll go wherever you lead. I'll do whatever happens."

And everything changed. I have peace. I have serenity. I have success beyond my wildest dreams.

All the art of living lies in the fine mingling of letting go and holding on.

Havelock Ellis

Doing nothing is sometimes one of the highest of the duties of man.

G.K. Chesterton

February 24

Gratitude

A grateful heart sees a glimpse of heaven in everything.

Mimi Novic

God gave you a gift of 86,400 seconds today. Have you used one to say thank you?

William Arthur Ward

Gratitude is love.
Unconditional.
It is not because we are better or have more than others.
Gratitude is total. All-encompassing. When we stop entirely and do gratitude, everything else falls away, and ceases to exist.
Gratitude is not judgemental.
It is simply – Gratitude.

True forgiveness is when you can say, "Thank you for that experience."

Oprah Winfrey

I will be calm. I will be mistress of myself.

Jane Austen

Fear

Of all the liars in the world, sometimes the worst are our own fears.

Rudyard Kipling

This is a doing – not a reading.

Fear. We all have fear, be it great or small, a lot of the time.

If it is a genuinely great all-consuming fear, for example, of death. A fear that wracks our bodies, one might ask, if my fear of dying is so dreadful that it causes me this much distress, then wouldn't death be an incredible relief? Just to let go and be free of the fear. Such freedom.

We do fear in our bodies. It then travels to our minds, and we throw on more twigs, increasing the blaze.

If you are one of the 99.98% who has fear at this moment, please go into it, in your body. It is usually in the stomach, though it can be anywhere or everywhere. Go into it. Feel it. Sense its blackness.

As you do this, fear ceases to be specific. It is just fear. Raw fear. It has nothing to do with the reality of the situation. It is simply fear. Go right into its centre. Begin to let in a glimmer of light. [Remember, this is a doing, not a reading.] Let the light expand. Let it begin to dissolve. Become light.

Let it start to float away. To disappear. Take in a deep breath. Let it fill you with light.

Let the light fill you and radiate out of you.

Smile. Say "Thank you". Enjoy being you.

Remembering that I'll be dead soon is the most important tool I've ever encountered to help me make the big choices in life. Almost everything – all external expectations, all pride, all fear of embarrassment or failure – these things just fall away in the face of death, leaving only what is truly important.

Steve Jobs

February 26

Learning

Anyone who stops learning is old, whether at twenty or eighty. Anyone who keeps learning stays young.

Henry Ford

People talk about, groan about, and complain that it's Groundhog Day. Blah. Blah. Blah.

But I think they are missing the point. The opportunities of Groundhog Day are so vast and wonderful.

Just think for a few moments of the time you waste every day doing the same thing or doing nothing. And imagine the fantastic new dimensions you could add to your life if you spent – let's say – one hour a day learning something new instead of watching tv.

Or if you learnt a language or studied a new subject when commuting.

I have no idea what you could achieve with your life if you decided to discover new things or perfect something you used to be good at. But I'm sure that if you committed to it, you would be dazzled by your abilities a year from now.

One hour per day of study in your chosen field is all it takes. One hour per day of study will put you at the top of your field within three years. Within five years, you'll be a national authority. In seven years, you can be one of the best people in the world at what you do.

Earl Nightingale

Secrets

Don't pee on my leg and tell me it's raining.

Judge Judy Sheindlin

Sometimes, just sometimes, we do something... that well... we think we'll get away with. We are human, after all. And even if we cannot, at this moment, think of a single instant in our lives when we did that, somewhere we know that we have.

"So what?" you may say. "It didn't hurt anyone."

No, quite possibly not. No one except ourselves. We knew we had taken the bigger slice – or the smaller one, believing that no one would notice.

No one except ourselves.

And no, maybe that didn't matter... but... if we did it, and we noticed, then it did matter.

It mattered to our core self-image. And maybe there are much bigger things that we do or don't do that really disturb our self-image and self-respect.

So, if we want to feel genuinely, quietly, and honestly good about ourselves, then we want to keep the small things we do clean. Then it will be easier to change and accept our more significant challenges.

Just because you can't see it doesn't mean it's not there.

John Alejandro King

I like dogs that bark a little. The silent ones scare me.

Marty Rubin

February 28

Loneliness

Loneliness and the feeling of being unwanted is the most terrible poverty.

Mother Teresa

There are moments when we feel alone. Lost even. Abandoned.

A wave of quiet, or not so quiet, emotion flows through us. We long for, although we may not verbalise it like this, we long for a hug.

It is natural. It is human. We want to allow ourselves these moments without feeling less than, or for that matter, diving into them and embracing despair.

If when we recognise it, acknowledge it, and accept that it is something that is happening, we want to go inside and give ourselves a hug.

Feel the warmth of the hug.

Let the traces of a smile begin to curl our lips.

Be grateful. Grateful for the hug.

Enjoy it and move into being.

The longer one is alone, the easier it is to hear the song of the earth.

Robert Anton Wilson

We are all sentenced to solitary confinement inside our own skins, for life.

Tennessee Williams

Self-Image

I used to be self-conscious about my height, but then I thought, fuck that, I'm Harry Potter.

Daniel Radcliffe

You will act like the sort of person you conceive yourself to be.

Maxwell Maltz

By and large, throughout our childhood, we've collected a vast number of other people's opinions about us. They gave us labels and nicknames. They said or implied that we weren't good enough, that we would not achieve... And so there they are, burnt into our minds, ready to trip us up and make us feel less than...

Our egos have a field day with these ideas, pulling them out of the box and belittling us.

Realising that our ego is using them to damage us, we can learn to reject the ego's attempts to undermine us. We can go inside to the other voice, the voice of love and find the courage to change the way we look at and behave in the world.

No one ever told me I was pretty when I was a little girl. All little girls should be told they're pretty, even if they aren't.

Marilyn Monroe

You can't have everything. Where would you put it?

Steven Wright

Your

thoughts

create

Your

reality

Change

Nothing changes until the pain of remaining the same is greater than the pain of changing.

Jim Burns

We all want to make changes in our lives.

Almost everyone does, be it minor or significant. But we travel along without changing, just accepting our shortcomings (if that's the right word).

We seldom change anything until the pain is significant enough in whatever form it takes.

We think I must eat less, or I must remember to do this or not to do that. I must... I should... I've got to...

But the pain is not enough to inspire us to take the necessary action.

We have to "want" change for it to have any chance of working. Whenever we think about what we want to change, remember to say, "I want to do it".

I have discovered a way to make changes. Go into the current behaviour deeply and feel the pain it causes. Experience the pain that it causes in your body.

Then say, "Enough. It is time to do this differently." Visualise life with the new behaviour in place.

You may have to do this many times, but the new behaviour gathers strength until it becomes the new automatic response.

Go for it. You can do it if you want to.

Intelligence is the ability to adapt to change.

Stephen Hawking

Selfishness

Your conscience is the measure of the honesty of your selfishness. Listen to it carefully.

Richard Bach

A girl was permanently ill, bedridden most of the time. Her mother looked after her every need.

When she was in her early 40's, her mother died.

After five days, she got up. She discarded her illnesses. She found a job and supported herself, living without troubles, difficulties, or diseases.

Dreadful story.

How could anyone do something like that?

And yet, if we look honestly and sincerely at our lives and relationships, are there things we do that take advantage of others?

It is worth considering, because obviously we would not want to do that. Would we?

One day, you'll notice something different, and if you take advantage of that moment, you will be what you exactly needed to be.

Auliq Ice

Every small, unselfish action nudges the world into a better path. An accumulation of small acts can change the world.

Robin Hobb

Disruption

Fucking two things up at the same time isn't multitasking.

Dick Masterson

Sometimes we dash, helter-skelter, from one thing to the next and back to the one before last, inflicting more uncompleted tasks like a headless chicken, wondering why we can no longer pick up grain with our beaks.

Oh, how the ego loves this. The more disruption it causes in our lives, the happier it is.

I can tell you, from a mountain of self-experience and what I've learned from others, that our ego is not our friend.

It is possible that you don't know that your ego is not your ally. And it will never even allow you to consider this possibility if it has you completely in its grasp.

It screams to us stop, behave, lie, and fail. It doesn't tell us directly to fail, it's too clever for that, but it creates problems and worries for us at every turn.

Suppose we can learn to stop it. Even for a few seconds and review our turmoil. Discarding it bit by bit until we have a glimmer of peace.

If we can allow the still calmness from our heart to speak to us, then we can discover how to move forward with gentle elegance. Then we can enjoy our life and focus on what is truly important to us.

Yes, and how many deaths will it take till he knows that too many people have died.

Bob Dylan

Care

The closest thing to being cared for is to care for someone else.

Carson McCullers

We are cared about. You are cared about.

Sometimes we go through our life without considering or noticing that we are cared about. We take things for granted and lose the opportunity to enrich our lives and the life of the person who has if only briefly, cared about us.

In the simplest example, when someone lets us into a stream of traffic, they are expressing their care for us.

And expressions of care go from that to deepest love and affection.

Take time now to go back to the past and recall a time when someone did something for you because they cared about you. Go into the event and feel it in your body now. Allow the feeling to grow and spread through your being.

Every time we do something caring for others, every time we recognise someone being caring towards us, we strengthen caring in our lives. We increase its flow.

The more we give, the more we will receive.

It is the time you have wasted for your rose that makes your rose so important.

Antoine de Saint-Exupéry

The bond that links your true family is not one of blood, but of respect and joy in each other's life.

Richard Bach

The Present

The only joy in the world is to begin.

Cesare Pavese

He who kisses the joy as it flies,
Lives in eternity's sunrise.

William Blake

It's the little moments that we miss. Millions and millions and millions of them. They flit by. Unnoticed and of no benefit to us because we miss them. Shame.

So preoccupied with what's coming or not coming. So absorbed by all the things that happened or didn't happen.

If we look honestly at the past, we'll see that despite all the things we thought we ought do to make it better, 99% of our insane ranting we totally ignored. We haven't done anything about any of it.

And the same is true about our fears and worries of the future, 99% of them never even happen. But we make sure that we are suffering because of them now. After all, why wait for the future when we can give ourselves a hard time now?

So?

Well?

If we are here, now, fully, we can enjoy peace. And armed with that peace, we can do whatever is required of us in the next now.

No one saves us but ourselves. No one can and no one may.
We ourselves must walk the path.

Buddha

Harvesting

We must give more in order to get more. It is the generous giving of ourselves that produces the generous harvest.

Orison Swett Marden

On lovely days I harvest "Beautiful" and "Gorgeous".

As I pass people, I say, "Lovely day", and lots of them reply "Beautiful" and "Gorgeous".

On less good days, I harvest smiles.

I smile at people as we pass each other, and about 50% of them smile back.

It makes me feel so good.

It makes them feel good too.

Get out there and spread joy.

Get out there and harvest.

The thankful receiver bears a plentiful harvest.

William Blake

Opportunities come infrequently. When it rains gold, put out a bucket, not a thimble.

Warren Buffet

Inactivity

The hardest thing is to do nothing and do it well.

Marty Rubin

Doing nothing is very hard to do... you never know when you're finished.

Leslie Nielsen

Doing nothing.

Why? Because we don't feel well, because we genuinely need a rest, or even because we just don't want to do anything.

Guilt? Self-persecution?

Or do we suffer from the inability to stop?

Perhaps we don't allow ourselves to have a break, even when it's the right thing to do, because we don't want to set an example of idleness.

However, the truth is that there are times when just stopping is a good, maybe even the best, idea.

And so, when we think of not doing things, it is a good idea to accept that and wait until we are connected and energized.

Our ego will undoubtedly find reasons to criticise us, whether we do anything or not, so we are well-advised to tell it to "Shut up".

If you're not able to sit down and do nothing for one hour, you're addicted to stimulation, and you will never attain true happiness.

Robert Celner

Tension is who you think you should be. Relaxation is who you are.

Chinese Proverb

March 8

Sheep

The shepherd always tries to persuade the sheep that their interests and his own are the same.

Stendhal

People are sheep. TV is the shepherd.

Jess C. Scott

People think that sheep are stupid because they won't do what the farmer wants.

The sheep thinks, "He wants me to go through that gate, but I don't trust him. I'll go towards the gate and then nip off in another direction just as I get to the gate. That'll fool him. Ha. I don't trust what might happen through the gate."

I don't know if you've ever had the pleasure of travelling on the Underground/Subway during rush hour? I've always thought there would be a public outcry if we treated animals in this way.

A mass of humans is far more stupid than sheep.

We do not need to follow the herd. We do not have to be bullied into doing things against our beliefs. We do not have to buy into the fear that walks hand in hand with more fear down our streets.

We are free. Or we can be free if we choose to be. We can claim our independence.

The most courageous act is still to think for yourself. Aloud.

Coco Chanel

Love

All you need is love.

Lennon & McCartney

Only peace can save the world, and only love can create a liveable earth!

Mehmet Murat Ildan

I can choose.

I can choose love.

I can find in my heart the light and feel the love flowing through my body. All my troubled thoughts disintegrate as love and peace flow through me.

I can be at peace. Untroubled.

But it does not last for long. My ego quickly rallies itself and starts beating its drum of worry and fear. Louder and louder. So easy to allow the struggle into my day and my life.

But.

I can choose peace.

The more often I do, the better my life is.

You'll never find peace of mind until you listen to your heart.

George Michael

You find peace not by rearranging the circumstances of your life, but by realising who you are at the deepest level.

Eckhart Tolle

Change

Not everything that is faced can be changed, but nothing can be changed until it is faced.

James Baldwin

In the movie Groundhog Day, there is a homeless guy who dies. Bill Murray gives him money, feeds and looks after him. But he just keeps dying, and there's nothing that Bill Murray can do about it. He dies.

Some things simply happen in our lives. And however hard we try to change their course, we cannot.

Not just the people in our lives who die. But the events and their consequences too. There is no point in beating ourselves up or despairing.

Meaningful, lasting change only happens when the pain of the status quo finally outstrips the fear or the anticipated pain of the change we seek.

Davin Taylor-Klaus

Thoughts

Our way of thinking creates good or bad outcomes.

Stephen Richards

No one can put a negative thought into our mind. Yes, they may say something that starts a thought, but what we do with it is totally up to us.

We can accept or reject it. We can water and feed it. Or we can pluck it out, and replace it with positives, self-belief, and love.

The more we approach life with a "Yes I can" attitude, the more we achieve. And with greater ease.

This includes everything we expose ourselves to. Watching the news, reading about the awful things man is doing. If we are bathing in negativity in any way, it cripples our ability to be positive, achieve what we want, and believe in ourselves.

We want to focus on the positives and pat ourselves on the back whenever we have a success. We want to be proud of all our achievements and believe that we can.

Whenever you want to achieve something, keep your eyes open, concentrate and make sure you know exactly what it is you want. No one can hit their target with their eyes closed.

Paulo Coelho

Fear

The attempt to escape the pain is what creates more pain.

Gabor Maté

Our negative emotions are all fear. And are created by our ego.

As long as the ego is succeeding in this. It is achieving its aim of controlling us.

It does not want us to be happy. "That's not true!" it shouts. But it lies. For when we are happy, it loses control of us.

All fears are the same. They may wear a mass of different labels, but they all come from the same place within us.

If we look at the cause of our fear, we can choose to process our situation from a new perspective.

The moment we go into the peace and love of our inner being, fear ceases to exist. The ego is silenced. If only for a few moments.

We can act and react with calmness and with love. We can take the strength of love into our thoughts and our day.

We forge the chains we wear in life.

Charles Dickens

March 13

Possessions

Are you rich or do you just have money?

Frank Sonnenberg

I love things made out of animals. It's just so funny to think of someone saying, "I need a letter opener. I guess I'll have to kill a deer".

David Sedaris

Have you ever noticed that people who are truly secure and content with themselves do not need to buy or own expensive things to prove their wealth?

From childhood onwards, there is so much peer pressure to have a new thing. To wear the right clothes and prove that we are better than "okay" on social media.

None of this accounts for anything. It is all meaningless. It does not make us happy. Yes, we may have a few minutes of delight, but then it is gone, we are back on the treadmill trying to prove that we are not "less than".

When we learn to accept, enjoy, and love ourselves, we stop chasing ways to prove the unprovable, we can have peace, serenity, and happiness.

Let go of the hunt. Love yourself. You are good enough as you are.

You only truly possess that which you cannot lose in a shipwreck.

Abu Hamid Al Ghazali

You can't have everything. Where would you put it?

Steven Wright

Trials

Life gives you what you settle for.

James Serengia

We all have trials. I know we do.

What is important (I guess) is how we deal with them.

My wife has a real job, so I do most of the cooking.

About three or four times a year, my mother-in-law comes and stays. Often but not always, she re-arranges the kitchen cupboards. Before she goes, being a considerate mother, she says to my wife, "I've moved some things around in the kitchen for you so that they are easier to find and use. I know you'll see sense in the changes." And then she leaves.

She doesn't tell me.

Quite often, my wife doesn't tell me.

So, I go to the kitchen cupboards, and everything has changed. It takes an age to get it all back in order.

Looking at it now, I realise I should have said something the first time she did it, but I didn't want to upset her. She had, after all, been helpful.

And now... Well, I don't want to upset her.

I have dreamt about going to her house and moving everything around in her kitchen, but that would be spiteful.

Why do I mention any of this? To give you, perhaps, a gentle smile. And also, so that you can realise that you are not the only person who has trials. (Hurrah for that!)

Education is not the learning of the facts but the training of the mind to think.

Albert Einstein

Listening

Never miss a good chance to shut up.

Will Rogers

"Yak, yak, yak" goes our mind. Even when we are silent. Even when we are listening.

There are times – especially with people we genuinely love – when we listen. But by and large, we are listening with our heads, weighing everything up, before replying.

Honest, real listening is done with our hearts, not our heads. And when they finish speaking, we open our mouths, and words come out.

That is listening with the heart and then speaking from it.

For most of us, that only happens by accident.

On reflection, we think, "Where did that come from? I can't have said that." And even, "I would never have dared to say that."

So, if when we are in a conversation, we make a conscious decision to turn off the inner "yak", and allow our hearts to listen, we give ourselves wholly to the exchange, then the wisdom of our heart will be heard more often.

Most of the successful people I've known are the ones who do more listening than talking.

Bernard Baruch

Challenge

Life throws challenges, and every challenge comes with rainbows and lights to conquer it.

Amit Ray

The challenge is... the real challenge is... saying "Thank you".

We have troubles, small, medium, vast, unbearable. Situations and people in our lives that fling open the trapdoor to hell. (Hopefully – not that bad.) But whether small or great they begin to crush the life and light out of us.

Every tiny little trouble diminishes us. Makes us less. So you don't need to be a rocket scientist to realise that our more significant challenges are more damaging to us.

We become greater by living through our challenges grow, learn. So... if we say "thank you" to them, it instantly changes the relationship, they diminish, and we grow stronger.

So, even if you don't feel like it or want to tell me to go to hell, do it.

Say thank you inwardly. And say it again and again. Things will change. I promise you.

The strong-minded rise to the challenge of their goals and dreams. The weak-minded become haters.

Steve Maraboli

Every challenge you face today makes you stronger tomorrow. The challenge of life is intended to make you better, not bitter.

Roy T. Bennett

Sleep

Nothing can bring you peace but yourself.

Ralph Waldo Emerson

When we lie down in bed on our way to sleep, our bodies are not relaxed. There is still a tension holding everything in place.

To speed our journey to sleep, we want to relax our head entirely into the pillow and then our body totally, so that we can feel our body's weight sinking into the mattress.

Then relax our jaw, our face.

Relax our eyelids, our eyes. Allow them to sink into the position they have when we are asleep.

Bask in relaxation without thought.

Sleep comes so elegantly.

How beautiful it is to do nothing and then rest afterwards.

Spanish Proverb

Laughter

In the sweetness of friendship, let there be laughter and sharing of pleasures. For in the dew of little things does the heart find its morning and is refreshed.

Khalil Gibran

When I was young, I could not laugh at myself. Make fun of me, and you had an enemy for life. Or at least for the next hour or so.

I've changed, I might still struggle if you really took the piss out of me, but I can laugh.

I laugh a lot. I laugh when things go wrong. I find humour easily.

I do not take myself or the world seriously. That doesn't mean that I don't succeed in what I'm doing. It doesn't mean that I don't get on with what needs to be done, which is perhaps what people call taking things seriously.

It means most of all that I take the stress out of things. I enjoy what I do. I help others to enjoy what they do. And we all look for opportunities to laugh. It's good. Life's good. Life is fun.

Laughter is the shortest distance between two people.

Victor Borge

Attitude

It's all in the mind.

George Harrison

There is a story about someone who asked three stonemasons building Notre Dame Cathedral what they were doing. The first said he was working, the second said he was a stonemason, and the third said, "I am building a cathedral."

It is an excellent question to ask ourselves as we go about our lives.

And to decide which answer reflects our attitude.

And perhaps, to get more joy from what we do, change our approach to it.

If the doors of perception were cleansed everything would appear to man as it is, Infinite. For man has closed himself up, till he sees all things thro' narrow chinks of his cavern.

William Blake

Doing

*You don't learn to walk by following rules. You learn by
doing, and by falling over.*

Richard Branson

Sometimes we have so, so much to do. We never stop. As
soon as we finish one thing, two more are added to the
endless array of things to be done.

We battle on, doing and doing, trudging through the day,
exhausted.

And if we stop?

Well, "Guilt" has a field day! Bells and whistles. "You're
not good enough." "You're useless." Such a quandary.

And no, of course, you can't ask anyone to help you!
Don't be ridiculous!

However, pacing ourselves, looking after ourselves, and
nourishing ourselves mentally and physically enables us to
do more in less time.

People say, "I don't have time to meditate." But ironically,
when we meditate, we have more time and accomplish more.

And having a proper relax, with a cup of tea and a nibble,
enables us to get on with what needs doing more efficiently
and with more energy.

We can achieve so much more with a gentle smile on our
face and a light heart than we ever will when scowling in a
cloud of blackness.

*I'm having fun. I'm being myself. I'm doing what I love.
That's all that matters.*

James Charles

March 21

Living

Life is long if you know how to use it.

Seneca

Do we know how to use it? Do you? Do I? There are, hopefully, times when we do, when we immerse ourselves fully in what we are doing.

And there are times too, when we need a break from the immersion, just to veg out. But sadly, I suspect, most of us very rarely involve our whole being in the act of living in the now. We squander our time like children running through fields, plucking the heads off the flowers, and throwing them away.

So good to pick just one flower, or sit and become one with the flower. The flower is not thinking about tomorrow or yesterday. It is in the present moment.

Stop acting as if life is a rehearsal.

Live this day as if it were your last. The past is over and gone. The future is not guaranteed.

Wayne Dyer

Visualising

You can't depend on your eyes when your imagination is out of focus.

Mark Twain

For the last forty or so years, before going on any journey, I have gone into a meditative state, visualised the journey, in whatever detail I know, and seen myself arriving safely.

On two occasions, I was unable to see myself finishing the journey.

After several attempts, I set off anyway. I'm human. I'm impetuous.

On the first occasion, I got three-quarters of my way home when my radiator emptied, and I couldn't go any further.

The second time was rather more exciting. I was driving south in the fast lane of the M1. An Audi Quatro, coming north in the fast lane, left the road. It flew sideways over the crash barrier, hitting a lamppost with its roof. Bits flew off it into my car. I had a broken windscreen, a punctured radiator, and a large number of holes in my bonnet.

I just managed to get home.

Now I no longer leave if I cannot complete the journey in my mind before I go.

If you can dream it, you can do it.

Walt Disney

You have to visualise a second or two ahead of your car, what line you are taking, what you are going to do, before you get there, because it comes too fast.

Emerson Fittipaldi

Forgiveness

It's not an easy journey, to get to a place where you forgive people. But it is such a powerful place, because it frees you.

Tyler Perry

There is an ancient Hawaiian practice of forgiveness called Ho'oponopono.

It is a mantra, and it translates to:

"I'm sorry, please forgive me. Thank you, I love you."

Repeat it to yourself several times, pausing after each time you say it.

Forgiveness starts with ourselves. Until we have forgiven ourselves, there can be no forgiveness. So, the mantra is directed to ourselves.

Forgive others not because they deserve forgiveness but because you deserve peace.

Jonathan Lockwood Huie

Argument

Don't raise your voice, improve your argument.

Desmond Tutu

Yesterday I had words, a row, and a confrontation with someone.

I rarely do this because it causes me distress, and I don't like it.

It caused her distress too. I apologised sincerely, though she wasn't interested in that. She was hanging onto her "Rightness", which I understand. I shall apologise again when I next see her, and I hope she will be feeling better by then. But if she insists on clinging to her hurt, there is nothing I can do. That is her choice.

I apologised because she was hurt, not because I thought what I had said was wrong. The rightness or wrongness of it is factual, not emotional.

This morning I awoke with physical discomfort in my head and abdomen because of her and the altercation. So, before I got up, I went into the pain in my head. A hard, dark block and I lightened it, softened it, lightened, and softened it more until it floated away.

I went into the knot in my stomach and filled it with brilliant white light. I saw the knots disintegrating and floating away too.

I did have to release the knot in my stomach a couple of times during the morning, but it's gone now. I can think of her and smile with love.

Take no thought of who is right or wrong or who is better than. Be not for or against.

Bruce Lee

Relax! Life is beautiful.

David L. Wolper

March 25

Peace

The meaning of life is to find your gift. The purpose of life is to give it away.

Pablo Picasso

The answer is in the stillness within.

So often, we dash and crash through our lives, oblivious of life's importance. We do not rate ourselves. We find it hard to accept the honest compliments we receive.

Perhaps that doesn't apply to you. But many who think it doesn't are deluded by their self-importance, which is probably worse.

The things that we can truly give away are the things that come from within us. These are not looking for rewards, acknowledgement, or accolades. They are simply passing the peace of our inner being to others. They receive it and are quietly changed because of it.

And so, if we want to do this more often, we want to learn to surrender our self-will and say, "I can't handle this, you do it", and hand it over.

Let the words and the love flow simply from us, out into the world.

Inner stillness is the key to outer strength.

Jared Brock

Depression

Because grey clouds hang heavy with misery, blue skies seem bluer.

Richelle E. Goodrich

The sky is always blue (during the day).
Beyond the clouds, it is blue.
Beyond the clouds, the sun shines.
Sometimes we forget.
Sometimes we allow ourselves to be swamped with the grey blackness in our lives. We fall into the "this'll never end" pity party.

Maybe you never go that low. I hope not. But there are days in most people's lives when they focus on the clouds and allow the dark into their minds.

And when that happens, we can take a breath, a deep conscious breath, and hold it in. And as we exhale, we allow our minds, our being, to float through the clouds into the beauty of the blue sky.

And repeat as often as necessary.
Bathe in the blue.
Shed the dark.
Remember that our life has been a constant journey of ups and downs, but we've always come through.

This too shall pass.
It will.

Complete people gaze into the blue sky above, plunge into the centre of the earth below, and run freely in the eight directions without even a change of mood.

Liezi

Searching

*Why do you so earnestly seek
the truth in distant places?
Look for delusion and truth
in the bottom of your own heart.*

Ryokan

We search for answers, for meaning.

Search, search, search.

What new thing, idea, way, holds the answer, the solution?

We fill ourselves with more and more knowledge in the hope of... what?... Enlightenment... (Hang on there, "Enlightenment is too much, that's unobtainable... even if I got close... I'm not worthy, I couldn't...")

But if that is the case, what are we looking for? Just a bit of peace, perhaps?

The trouble is that we become obsessed with the search. Even if we met the solution, we would dash on to the next thing, searching and searching.

Like a child who does not know about money, we are sent into a fantastic shop with a $100 note. But because he doesn't know he has money in his hand, he cannot buy anything.

We have always had light and peace from the moment we entered this body. The solution, our soul, spirit, and peace are within us. We can connect with it whenever we want to if we stop and choose to.

It has been said that man is a rational animal. All my life, I have been searching for evidence which could support this.

Bertrand Russell

Happiness

You will never be happy if you continue to search for what happiness consists of. You will never live if you are looking for the meaning of life.

Albert Camus

Ah, happiness.

So often, our happiness is dependent on other people, things, the weather, or the kind of work we do.

Perhaps that sentence should read, "So often our "unhappiness" is dependent on..."

We blame so many outside factors for dragging us down.

However, if we choose to control our minds, notice and experience the good rather than the bad, we can change everything.

Other people, our partner, that driver, that customer, cannot make us feel anything. We simply choose to allow them to. We create our feelings.

And so we can, if we decide to find the good rather than the bad, move through our day not allowing other people's crud to stick to us, but instead find something positive to focus on.

Therein lies the path to happiness.

It isn't what you have or who you are or where you are or what you are doing that makes you happy or unhappy. It is what you think about it.

Dale Carnegie

If only we'd stop trying to be happy, we could have a pretty good time.

Edith Wharton

Smile

Because of your smile, you make life more beautiful.

Thich Nhat Hanh

Do me a favour.
Just take a moment or three to clock how you are feeling
now inside and throughout your body.
And now.
Next favour.
Smile.
Bigger.
And now check how you feel.
Better eh!
So another smile, please.
Maybe even a chuckle.
Then the world is easier to face.
More than easier even.
So do yourself a favour.
Remember this.
And do it often.
Teach others.
Enjoy.

*A simple smile. That's the start of opening your heart and
being compassionate to others.*

Dalai Lama

*Use your smile to change the world; don't let the world
change your smile.*

Chinese Proverb

Giving

The best thing to do with the best things in life is to give them away.

Dorothy Day

A mother gave her son two shirts. He comes down wearing one, and she, enormously distressed, cries out, "What was wrong with the other one?"

My grandmother was very generous but never let go of anything she gave. If she came round to my house, she'd dash to look at the chair, or table she'd given me, to ensure I was looking after them properly.

I believe that when we give someone something, that's it. It is theirs. We have no right to monitor it. If we are watching it, we haven't given it.

People want to be allowed to get on with their lives without interference.

For it is in giving that we receive.

Saint Francis of Assisi

Choice

In any moment of decision, the best thing you can do is the right thing, the next best thing you can do is the wrong thing. The worst thing you can do is nothing.

Theodore Roosevelt

Some people believe that we choose the families we are born into and, therefore, the life we are in.

Whether you believe that or not, it is interesting to consider the question, "Why did I choose this?" and "What am I here to learn?"

And then perhaps the more important question of "How can I help others, on this journey? What am I learning, that I can use to impact other people positively."

We journey with them. They give us knowledge and strength that we can share.

We are our choices.

Jean-Paul Sartre

Easy does it

Wisdom

In the presence of eternity, the mountains are as transient as the clouds.

Robert Green Ingersoll

Everything in the universe that comes and goes is not real.

If you think of anything in your life that comes and goes, exists, and will cease to exist, you will see that its impermanence removes its meaning.

But within you, there is something that is always there.

If you go in and find it, you will realise it is always there. It has always been there. You will know that whatever happens, it will continue to be there.

This awareness will enable you to understand the unimportance of the things that come and go.

You will be liberated.

And from now on, the world will be different whenever you remember this.

We are awakened to the profound realisation that the true path to liberation is to let go of everything.

Jack Kornfield

Suffering

*To live is to suffer, to survive is to find some meaning in the
suffering.*

Friedrich Nietzsche

Most of us are in love with suffering.
(Most of us almost certainly includes you.)
But! But! But! Wait...

Choose one thing in your life that is not perfect. Now
think about how that makes you feel. Is the feeling good or
bad?

If it's bad, why are you choosing to feel bad? We have a
choice about how we feel about everything.

So much of the time, we choose the bad feeling. And we
do this because we are in love with suffering. We have honed
our ability to react in just such a way from infancy onwards.
And now here we are, choosing to continue to suffer.

But now, we can change our choice if we want to.
It is up to us, suffering or peace.
Difficult choice, eh?

*A man who fears suffering is already suffering from what
he fears.*

Michel de Montaigne

April 3

Meditation

Action is the antidote to despair.

Joan Baez

I have been meditating for the best part of 40 years.

Occasionally something has happened to alter my routine. I've gone on holiday, for example, and stopped meditating.

And then, when I got home, because it is no longer part of my routine, I've let it slip. And gradually, I've stop meditating.

Each time that has happened, some four to six weeks later, I've realised that my life has become grey and flat. Purposeless.

And I start to meditate again. Within 36 hours, the world has changed. It is as if someone has suddenly turned the lights on. I am alive again.

And the coincidences start happening again. I am in the right place at the right time to meet the person I didn't even know existed.

God provides the wind, but man must raise the sails.

St. Augustine

April 4

Relaxing

Don't underestimate the value of doing nothing, of just going along, listening to all the things you can't hear, and not bothering.

A. A. Milne

Relax your jaw.

There, and you did not even know that it was not relaxed. Now relax your shoulders, stomach, back, pelvis, legs, feet and toes. And now relax your neck and head.

Take a deep breath.

Hold it in.

Let it out ever so slowly.

Smile.

Say "Thank you" to yourself.

Give yourself a hug.

Kiss yourself.

Say, "I love you".

Repeat often.

Life isn't as serious as the mind makes it out to be.

Eckhart Tolle

Your mind will answer most questions if you learn to relax and wait for the answer.

William Burroughs

April 5

Sleep

We are such stuff
As dreams are made on, and our little life
Is rounded with a sleep.

William Shakespeare – The Tempest

The sleep gurus tell us we should shut out the light and sleep in blackness.

How very sad.

How very unromantic.

I sleep with the curtains open as wide as they can be.

I awake from time to time as I turn over in the night.

I look out at the sky with joy.

The moonlight smiling down at me with its silver beauty and or peeking through the scurrying clouds. The subtle changes in the sky's colour. The first glimmers of blue. The rain, the lightning and the wind throwing the branches around. I am always delighted by the little interruptions.

If you have been sleeping in blackness, adjusting may take a little time, but it is so worth it.

Don't say to yourself, "I can't sleep with the curtains open" or "I can't sleep with the light."

You know you have slept in light.

Instead, say, "I delight in being alive and part of everything."

Each night when I go to sleep, I die. And the next morning,
when I wake up, I am reborn.

Mahatma Gandhi

Self-belief

Never let success go to your head, and never let failure go to your heart.

Ziad K. Abdelnour

Two shoe salesmen went to a country in Africa and discovered that virtually nobody there wore shoes.

One salesman left, stating, "I can't sell shoes here. Nobody wears them."

The other salesman said, "Oh wow, this is fantastic. Nobody here wears shoes."

So, the question is, which salesman are you?

I was so sad because I had no shoes, until I met a man that had no feet. So I said, "Got any shoes you're not using?"

Steven Wright

Strangers

Fear makes strangers of people who would be friends

Shirley MacLaine

I like talking to strangers in the street, not deep conversations (usually) but quick exchanges.

I was standing next to a young man on a mobility scooter the other day, and I asked him cheerfully, "Can you do a wheelie in that thing?" He looked up and said, "It was doing a wheelie that put me in it."

Oops.

And as I am thinking about it again now, more oops. So I'll be more tactful in future.

But I shall talk to people whenever I can. When I give money to people I stand and chat with them, and find out how they are doing.

As you grow older you'll find that you enjoy talking to strangers far more than to your friends.

Joy Williams

Respect

Respect is a two-way street, if you want to get it, you've got to give it.

R. G. Risch

"Am I disturbing you?"

That is a question I ask, when I phone people.

I do not wish to intrude into their space when I am not welcome.

And I believe that it gives them time to prepare themselves for our conversation. It shows respect.

And I suspect it is more likely that they will engage in our conversation.

I do wish that more people would ask me that question.

[Answering the phone] Hello, this is a recording, you've dialled the right number, now hang up and don't do it again.

Frank Sinatra

One Thing

I've done the calculation, and your chances of winning the lottery are identical whether you play or not. The good news is that going blind is not going to make you as unhappy as you think it will. The bad news is that winning the lottery will not make you as happy as you expect.

Fran Lebowitz

One thing!

Just one thing at a time!

So often, our thoughts are like all the lottery balls bouncing violently and uncontrollably.

We grab one and start to consider it, then another comes along and smashes the first one away, consuming all our attention.

You will not believe this, but you control your mind. You choose how it works.

So here's the thing. Tell it to stop. Slow it right down, slow motion, press the pause button, so all the balls are hanging in their own space. Reach in and choose one ball.

Yes, just one.

Now consider and decide what you are going to do with that thought. How are you going to deal with it? What actions can you take now?

Other thoughts may jump in because they're connected to that thought, leave them. Their turn will come. Deal with the one thing.

Yes, this one thing. Write down (if you can) what you will do, and then do it. If more needs to be done, move the thought to that place in the future.

When you are done, if you want to, choose another ball.

Success demands singleness of purpose.

Vince Lombardi

Respect

Ignoring a child's disrespect is the surest guarantee that it will continue.

Fred G. Gosman

I was sitting with an old man, and he appeared to be picking his nose and flicking the bogeys on the carpet. Why am I trying to make this sound better than it was? He didn't appear to be. He was.

Finally, I asked him why he was doing it.

"Oh", he said, "out of kindness, it gives my wife or daughter something to hoover up."

There was a long pause, and I said, "But you wouldn't do that in someone else's house, would you?" He considered this slowly. "Well, not if they were watching."

I mention this to illustrate that we behave better with people we are less close to.

Why do we do this? Surely if we love someone, we should give them more respect than we give to strangers.

But the truth, sadly, is that so often, we allow all our worst traits out when we are at home. We do it without thinking. Or if we do think, we probably say some rubbish like, "Well, they know me, they know what I'm like, they don't mind, they can laugh at it."

All of which means I don't care enough to make an effort to behave well and treat them with the respect they deserve. This is who I am, and they'll have to put up with it.

So the question is, I guess, do I behave in such a selfish and unpleasant way?

When you tolerate disrespectful people, you disrespect yourself.

Wayne Gerard Trotman

Beliefs

Tell people there's an invisible man in the sky who created the universe, and the vast majority of them will believe you. Tell them the paint is wet, and they have to touch it to make sure.

George Carlin

Many people believe that their lives have a purpose and a destiny. That they are here for a reason.

And others believe that they are "here to get as much as they can" and are constantly driven to get more.

Whether you believe one of those or something completely different, I would like to suggest that what God wants for us is to love each other.

Indeed, if we approach what we are doing, the people we come into contact with and the world with love, our lives will be much better. We will have harmony and tranquility, which is good for everyone.

To believe in something, and not to live it, is dishonest.

Mahatma Gandhi

April 12

Choice

Choose your love. Love your choice.

Thomas S. Monson

I was on a plane, and the stewardess was making her announcements, "... the oxygen masks will fall, if you have children put your mask on before assisting them. If you have two children, you must decide which one you love the most."

So here is the question.

You are with your loved ones, family and friends, and they are all being swept away. Whom do you save? You can only save one.

Okay, so you've saved them. Now you can save one more. Go on until you have five people on the shore next to you.

How much time and love do you give to them on a day-to-day basis?

Is there more you want to be doing? What are you going to do about it?

The difficulty in life is the choice.

George A. Moore

I chose, and my world was shaken. So what? The choice may have been mistaken, the choosing was not. You have to move on.

Stephen Sondheim

April 13

Living

If you believe it will work out, you'll see opportunities. If you believe it won't, you'll see obstacles.

Wayne Dyer

I've had a lot of worries in my life, most of which never happened

Mark Twain

Throughout our lives we have arrived at times of challenge. Times when things seemed insurmountable. And yet we have gone through them, we are here, and most of our past problems are forgotten.

Surely there's a lesson there, if we were clever enough to absorb it.

Everything works out in the end, though not always how we think we want it to.

So, when we accept that, we can start discarding our worry and fear. We will know that things will almost certainly be better than we imagine because our imaginings are the work of our insane egos, finding new ways to increase our pain.

Have you noticed that we always create the worst possible outcomes in our mind, and they virtually never happen? So create good outcomes, and believe in them. Move towards them.

You cannot always control what goes on outside. But you can always control what goes on inside.

Wayne Dyer

Action

Smile in the mirror. Do that every morning, and you'll start to see a big difference in your life.

Yoko Ono

Sometimes we may feel inspired to do something or start doing something again that we used to enjoy. Walk, swim, paint, meditate, play an instrument, or do something nice with a child, partner or friend. (Please add your own.)

However, we seldom seem to have the time or the energy to do it.

The thoughts come and go, getting hazier and dimmer as time passes.

I know, I know, you are really busy, and if I had your life, I would find it hard too.

If you had a bow, an arrow, and a target, you would only hit the target by concentrating on it.

So if there is something that you want to do, do it today. Even if you can only spend five minutes doing it. Tomorrow you may find that the five minutes turns into six, ten, fifteen.

It'll get easier. You will find that you have more time to shed the drudge.

Don't stop. Starting again is incredibly hard, it's much easier to keep going.

Success is not final, failure is not fatal. It is the courage to continue that counts.

Winston Churchill

Sobriety

It's not what happens to you, but how you react to it that matters.

Epictetus

Here's a thought about yourself that you have probably never even considered.

Just because you're not drinking it does not mean that you are sober.

You shout, "But I am not an alcoholic!"

Quite honestly, that is irrelevant. It still does not mean that you are sober. And it goes without saying that people who are not sober, rarely consider that they may not be.

Being sober is a combination of a state of mind and being. It requires that we are not judgemental, nor indulging in anger or irritability, not self-righteous, not sorry for ourselves, not feeling less than, not feeling better than. It is a state of openness and love.

Everything is either love or fear. All emotions that are not love are fear. All actions that are not love are fear. Every negative thought is fear.

When we are sober, we are free from fear. We do not need to prove that we are right. We do not need to be loved. We do not have to do anything to change the way we feel. We are simply in a state of peace.

So there you go. Are you sober? Or do you have some work to do? I know that I do. But I also know that I do enjoy a lot of sobriety. It's good. I recommend it.

Openness of mind strengthens the truth in us and removes the dross from it, if there is any.

Mahatma Gandhi

Ribbons

What should I possibly have to tell you, oh venerable one?
Perhaps that you're searching far too much? That in all that
searching you don't find the time for finding?

Hermann Hesse

I would like to give you a present.

It is a length of ribbon. In fact, several lengths.

I tie my house keys on one, 15mm wide x 400mm long. I have written my phone number on the ribbon. Another shorter one is on my car keys, which also has my phone number on it.

Every pair of scissors in my house has a ribbon, making them easy to find.

It makes life so much easier to find things when they have a beautiful ribbon hanging from them.

Somebody asked me if I was looking for something. I am looking for everything.

Sam Sheridan

April 17

Satisfaction

How many times have you heard someone say
"If I had his money, I could do things my way."
But little do they know that it is so hard to find
One rich man in ten with a satisfied mind.

Joe "Red" Hayes & Jack Rhodes.

Oh, how we search for things in our lives. People, jobs and love, in the hope of achieving joy. Fulfilment. Peace. Happiness.

Oh, how we struggle.

And even when we realise that the next car, partner, doughnut, or drink will not satisfy us, we pursue them anyway.

How extraordinarily human we are.

How very sad we are to be caught up in something like that and be unable to let it go.

There is peace. There is oneness.

All we have to do is choose it. And do it again. And again.

I can't get no satisfaction, I can't get no satisfaction.
Cause I try and I try and try, and I try,
I can't get no, I can't get no.

Keith Richards, Mick Jagger

April 18

Frailty

The vagabond who's rapping at your door. Is standing in the clothes that you once wore.

Bob Dylan

Such a haunting image. A knife to the heart.

It touches me deeply because, although that hasn't happened to me, I feel completely immersed in the pain of the situation. The pain that they are both in. The pain that I am in.

It reveals my frailty and my inability to help the world. It exposes my shortcomings and the difficulties that confront me when I want to make changes to myself.

And maybe, just maybe, I can take myself by the hand and say, "Come on, we can do it. It's not impossible. Courage."

If you are lucky enough to find a way of life you love, you have to find the courage to live it.

John Irving

April 19

Courage

You can't wait until life isn't hard anymore before you decide to be happy.

Nightbirde

Nightbirde, a singer on America's Got Talent, has cancer. She has a 2% chance of survival, but as she says, "2% is not 0%, 2% is something, and I wish people knew how amazing it is".

I guess there is a lesson there for us all if we are courageous enough to bring it into our lives.

Sometimes even to live is an act of courage.

Lucas Annaeus Seneca

Sadly, after this writing, Nightbirde died in February 2022.

Openness

*It irritates me to be told how things have always been done.
I defy the tyranny of precedent. I cannot afford the luxury
of a closed mind.*

Clara Barton

It is so easy to close one's mind, to prevent any noises coming from the other person from entering our brain.

When we were teenagers, we wrote off vast swathes of people because we knew they were too old and boring, too stupid or not on the right wavelength.

Maybe reading this, you're thinking, "I don't do that", and if you don't, bravo! You are, indeed, an exception.

As we grow older, we probably become more tolerant of the people we look down on.

But it is so easy to start a conversation with someone having already written them off. One of the mistakes people often make is to think that others are too old. They could not possibly understand. Or that they are too young, how could they know anything?

It's good to be open, to be receptive.

A closed mind is a dying mind.

Edna Ferber

Pain

*Behind every beautiful thing
There is some kind of pain*

Bob Dylan

*All I can do is be me
Whoever that is.*

Bob Dylan

Sometimes, life is a field of pain, and we plod through it, dragging our foot out of this mud-hole, only to squelch it into the next.

It is interesting that when we are out of the pain, we have difficulty remembering it.

However, when we are in it, trying uselessly to pull ourselves up by our bootlaces, we cannot imagine it ever ending. And when people tell us that it will end, we are hard-pressed to believe them.

If we can look dispassionately back at our lives, there are almost certainly situations in the past that were worse than the one that we were in. And if we cannot think of any in our life, there are millions of awful things that have happened to others.

Like Aron Lee Ralston, whose arm got trapped by a falling boulder when he was hiking and after 127 hours, he managed to cut it off with a blunt knife before making his way home.

And you think you've got problems.

If pain must come, may it come quickly. Because I have a life to live, and I need to live it in the best way possible. If he has to make a choice, may he make it now. Then I will either wait for him or forget him.

Paulo Coelho

Adventure

Climb every mountain
Ford every stream
Follow every rainbow
Till you find your dream.

Rogers & Hammerstein

Would you like to come on an adventure?

Half of you have packed your bags and are already standing outside your house, whilst the rest of you have sunk more tightly into your chair, worrying about what you should take and whether it will rain.

It is interesting, isn't it. It changes how you feel inside when you process the question.

Nearly all of us would have better, fuller lives if we allowed more adventure in. By and large we are tethered to routine. Anything that is out of the norm is difficult to do. And even those of us who are open to adventures could do with more.

Discard your shackles. Choose at least one adventure that you will have this week. Don't cheat yourself out of life.

If you think adventure is dangerous, try routine. It's lethal.

Paulo Coelho

Action

There are nettles everywhere
but smooth green grasses are
more common still, the blue of
heaven is larger than the cloud.

Elizabeth Barrett Browning

Sometimes all the nettles seem to arrive at once, and we feel utterly overwhelmed. It's all too much. The temptation is to close down completely. To go and hide until they are all gone.

Although we know that won't happen. Nettles are here to be dealt with. We cannot hide from them.

However, we can only do one thing at a time. Multitasking is a myth. People who multitask achieve less than those who deal with one thing at a time.

So pick one of the challenges you face and focus only on that until you have done all the things you can with it right now. Then put it down and choose the next one to deal with. Oh, and congratulate yourself on what you have done.

No one can liberate you, for no one has bound you; you hold onto the nettle of worldly pleasures, and you weep for pain. The kite is pursued by the crows, so long as it carries the fish in its beak, it twists and turns in the sky trying to last, and it drops the fish. That moment it is free. So give up the attachment to the senses; then grief and worry can harass you no more.

Sri Sathya Sai Baba

April 24

Love

Love is an untamed force. When we try to control it, it destroys us. When we try to imprison it, it enslaves us. When we try to understand it, it leaves us feeling lost and confused.

Paulo Coelho

In the twilight years of their marriage (if that's what it's called), one of my parents said to me, "I can't believe how he/she has put up with me all these years."

I genuinely don't know which parent said it. And they always presented a united front to me, so I cannot think, "it could only be my Mum/my Dad who said that."

So here is my dilemma, if two humans who appear to get along can be thinking that, then what the hell is going on?

And then you think about the couples who do not even appear to be getting on.

And one arrives at the question, "Why are they together?"

I have no idea about your circumstances, but I know it does not feel right for people to stay together when their time has run out.

Of course, they have fear and laziness battling to keep them together.

But really?

Really?

It's ridiculously easy to fall in love, what's hard is to sustain that love for life.

Abhijit Naskar

Ego

The critical voice is not your own.

Amelia Kinkade

Two voices. Two voices in our heads.

One so loud, barking insanities at us, finding fault, criticising us, and putting us down.

There's a story about a man who lost his keys one night in his garden. A friend saw him and asked, "Do you want some help?" They searched together. After a while, the friend asked, "Where exactly did you drop them?" "Over there," he replied, pointing to a dark corner of the garden. "Then why on earth are we looking over here?" "Well, it's light here, so it's easier to search."

Silly? Yes. But that is precisely what our ego does. It will do whatever it can to help us. Except find the keys.

But. Here's the thing, there is another voice. A still, quiet voice. It is within us – and it is there to help us.

That is the voice we want to cultivate and learn to be in touch with. It will show us the way. It is so tremendously powerful. We want to learn to have a deep and trusting relationship with it.

There is a voice inside of you.
 That whispers all day long,
"I feel that this is right for me,
I know that this is wrong."
No teacher, preacher, parent, friend
Or wise man can decide
What's right for you – just listen to
The voice that speaks inside.

Shel Silverstein

There is a God part in you. The consciousness. The pure Self. Learn to listen to the voice of that Power.

Amit Ray

Doing

If it matters how you do it
And how you do it, it's your thing
If it matters which way you go
That's your way to go.

Van Morrison

Oh, the struggle of doing the right thing, or the wrong thing for that matter. The effort of doing. Of deciding.

In the final analysis, what is important is doing. It's getting up out of the chair and doing.

Doing is better than not doing. Not doing is capitulating before you've even started. We want to be doers. We want to take the world and shake it. We want to take ourselves out and surprise ourselves. It's so very, very easy to do nothing.

So sad to look back upon our lives regretting that we didn't take risks. If we make a mistake, we are at least doing and can do the next thing. If we are in our chair, well, that's where we are, just waiting for someone to nail the lid on.

It's not because things are difficult that we dare not venture. It is because we dare not to venture that things are difficult.

Seneca

Sorry

Does Hallmark make a "Sorry I tried to drink your blood and touched you in a vaguely inappropriate manner" card? I settled for "How much do you remember?"

Molly Harper

I'm sorry.

How often is that the truth? Yes, we may be feeling guilty. More often, if we delve, it means sorry I got found out or sorry that you noticed.

Oh, and it also means, sorry, okay then, I won't do that for a while, or until I think that you won't notice, or till I hope you've forgotten, or until I think I can get away with it again, or until I'm drunk or stoned, and I really could not give a f*ck.

So there you are.

Very rarely is it the truth.

And when you think about it, if you ever do it again, it means "I lied! I am not sorry! I don't care!"

So do not say I'm sorry unless you will never do it again.

Or have the decency to say, "I'm sorry, I'm going to do it again. I can't help myself. That is the pathetic sort of human being I am."

I'm sorry if this all seems a little rushed and desperate. It is.

Chuck Palahniuk

Some apologies are like giving a bomb that is about to explode as a peace offering.

Mokokoma Mokhonoana

Sorry, I painted the word "Twat" on your garage door.

David Shrigley

Your Body

If you listen to your body when it whispers, you won't have to hear it scream.

Pilates saying

Before we get a headache, back pain or most physical troubles, our body whispers gently to us that it is time to stop or change what we are doing.

And yet we nearly always ignore it and carry on. Staring at the screen, lifting, lugging whatever we are moving, or even sitting badly.

If, what a big word "if" is. If we learn to stop and make changes, we can avoid unnecessary trouble.

We can go into our headache and dissolve it before it develops. We can change how we do things, and often just a short rest and a more diligent approach prevents the pain from developing. And if we have been sitting for more than forty-five minutes, our body deserves movement, even if it's just a stroll around our desk.

Our bodies are our gardens to which our wills are gardeners.

William Shakespeare – Othello

Distraction

I need something – the distraction of another life – to alleviate fear.

Bret Easton Ellis

When I was young, 6,7,8 years old, I don't remember, I had a toothache. I sat on my bed, whacking my head against the wall as hard as possible to counteract the toothache.

It seems extraordinary to me that a small boy could work out how to alleviate one pain by creating another more significant pain.

When I think about it, in many ways, we are still doing something like that in our lives today.

When we are suffering, rather than dealing with the cause of our troubles, we search for an alternative to distract us from the pain. The choice may not be an obvious creation of pain – like the headbanging – but it is not good.

Whether we use drugs, alcohol, shopping, eating, excessive exercise, sex, porn, computer games, gambling, anger, self-pity or anything else, it makes no difference to the source of the problem. And it is no more effective than banging our heads.

If we want the pain to go away, we have to deal with the source itself and not try to hide it with something else.

This I do being mad:
Gather baubles about me,
Sit in a circle of toys, and all the time
Death beating the door in.

Edna St Vincent Millay

Challenge

Do not go gentle into that good night,
Old age should burn and rave at close of day.
Rage, rage against the dying of the light.

Dylan Thomas

Although I am probably in the last quarter of my life, I do not feel that this poem only talks to the aged.

It seems to me that the young and the middle-aged want to rage against the dying of the light.

It is so easy at any age to start the process of withdrawal. To do less than one did or could do. To have fewer adventures.

Of course, unless you were brought up with a spirit of adventure, you may never have experienced it, except perhaps a brief adolescent rebellion.

Do not be like most people who stop living in their mid-20s and spend the rest of their lives waiting for their bodies to catch them up.

Challenge yourself. Get out there and live.

The secret of genius is to carry the spirit of the child into old age, which means never losing your enthusiasm.

Aldous Huxley

Forgive

Completely

Perception

To get the full value of joy, you must have someone to divide it with. After all these years, I see that I was mistaken about Eve in the beginning; it is better to live outside the Garden with her than inside it without her.

Mark Twain

Things are not how they appear to us.

"Things" appear in the dimensions we have set for them. All our life and training throughout the ages has given us our current viewpoints.

"They" have decided what we should laugh at, what makes us cringe or fear, and what we find arousing, disgusting, or acceptable.

And if you ask ten other people their views, they will undoubtedly differ from yours. And yet we continue to delude ourselves that everyone sees things as we do.

We can never judge the lives of others because each person knows only their own pain and renunciation. It's one thing to feel that you are on the right path, but it's another to think that yours is the only path.

Paulo Coelho

One of the symptoms of an approaching nervous breakdowns is the belief that one's work is terribly important.

Bertrand Russell

May 2

Normality

Normality is death.

Theodor Adorno

It is interesting, isn't it, that we do not aspire to be normal. We almost certainly look down on those whom we think of as normal. We believe they are less than.

There may be moments of strife in our lives when we wish we were normal. But only fleetingly.

I mean, what do ordinary people do, for god's sake? Drink tea and look out of the window? Have average cars, which they clean on Sunday? Take their shoes off when they go indoors? Put the covers down on the toilet when they've finished in there? I don't know...

I know I've never been normal, and it is only at moments like this when I confess, that it troubles me.

Go on, go out, be daring and outrageous.

Enjoy.

I have the normal complement of anxieties, neuroses, psychoses, and whatever else – but I'm absolutely nothing special.

Clive Barker

The bible tells us to love our neighbours, and also to love our enemies; probably because they are generally the same people.

G. K. Chesterton

"Normal" is just a setting on your dryer.

Patsy Clairmont

May 3

Control

Although the world is full of suffering, it is full also of the overcoming of it.

Helen Keller

True love is built on free will and free choice, not control and manipulation.

Ken Poirot

I'll tell you what makes us tense and uncomfortable. Or at least, I'll let you know one of the reasons. It's when people do not do what we, (very reasonably) want them to do. When we can't control them, it is easy to react with hurt and anger and inflict pain on ourselves and them if we can.

Interestingly, there are (or can be) two ways to process what is happening, what they're doing, what we are doing, and how we want it to go.

The first comes from the ego, who shouts orders and stamps its feet like an angry sergeant major. It is deafening and abusive and causes pain whenever it can.

The other comes from the gentleness in our heart, who does not need discipline to succeed. It wants what is best for us and everyone involved. It wants peace. And the things it suggests are nearly always right if we would but listen.

You always seek to control others when you are not in full ownership of yourself.

Cicely Tyson

Living

Here is the test to find out whether your mission on earth is finished. If you're alive, it isn't.

Richard Bach

We all have down days or times, even if they are only fleeting.

Times when our life, and our being seems to lack purpose. Life looks like a dirty carpet unwinding endlessly before us. We want to get off, go and hide, and sit in an armchair with a blanket over our head.

We want some proof that we exist. Someone to call us and tell us we matter.

Please.

Something.

Anything.

And for all the struggles to vanish and to have a no-demand cuddle.

We can be surrounded by people and action and still feel as isolated as the junkie alone in his squalid room.

Just because we are in the world, surrounded by people making demands on us, it does not stop us from feeling completely isolated. That is probably the worst type of isolation.

It is important to admit it to ourselves and take the time to talk honestly and slowly with someone.

Then we can enjoy travelling through our lives again.

The worst cruelty that can be inflicted on a human being is isolation.

Sukarno

May 5

Blame

A man gets discouraged many times, but he is not a failure until he begins to blame somebody else and stops trying.

John Burroughs

There was a time when I moved into a flat on my own, after living in a crowded house. Several months later, I was in the shower, and I reached out for the shampoo, it wasn't there.

"Who's moved the shampoo?" I shouted. And as the words fell to the floor like escaping water, I realised that it had to have been me.

How quick we are to blame. (Or is it just me? Am I the only one?)

And how comfortable for us when we can shift the blame to someone else because we know we are innocent. I throw that story and thought out for you to consider.

It's always easy to blame others. You can spend your entire life blaming the world, but your successes or failures are entirely your own.

Paulo Coelho

Decisions

If someone offers you an amazing opportunity, but you are not sure you can do it, say yes – then learn how to do it later.

Richard Branson

Are you a "Yes" person or a "No" person? If a good friend called you now and asked, "What are you doing this weekend?" Is your reaction one of caution or enthusiasm, and that's before they've even made a suggestion? Let's assume for the moment that you have no plans for the weekend.

Do you answer their question with "Nothing", or do you hedge your bets with a "not much" or perhaps "this and that, why?"

Are you already putting up little flags to avoid committing yourself?

So then comes their big follow-up question, how do you fancy... coming into the country and walking halfway up that mountain? Or come to a concert? Or come skydiving with me? Or come and spend the day with X, who's in hospital?

What we are looking for here is your initial response. Is it "yes, let's do it" or "how can I say no?"

We are not discussing the pros and cons of any suggestions, just your initial gut feeling. Many of us have an automatic reaction of caution and refusal.

If you are one of them, life might become more fun if you moved into the "yes" let's do it, group. You can still refuse if that becomes your reaction, but you will have stopped putting the automatic brakes on your life.

Dare to be vulnerable, walk outside without your armour on and say YES to your heart.

Alaric Hutchinson

Freedom

We don't heal in isolation, but in community.

S. Kelley Harrell

Fear is the path to the dark side. Fear leads to anger, anger leads to hate, hate leads to suffering.

Yoda

The Covid-19 pandemic led most of us into some degree of isolation. And isolation is so incredibly harmful. When we lock ourselves away, we begin to die. It affects every part of our being.

The fear that has swept the world is indescribably awful. The long-term effects of fear are far worse than any illness. The insanity of fear is worse for us than death. With death, there is peace. With fear, there is horror.

It's so vital that we discard all the elements of fear and join our beautiful fellow beings and rejoice at our freedom.

Be free.
Be alive.
Be.
Be in the world.
Be.
Enjoy.
Share joy.

Freedom is just another word for nothing left to lose.
Nothing don't mean nothing honey, if it ain't free.

Janice Joplin

May 8

Events

It all begins and ends in your mind. What you give power to has power over you.

Leon Brown

When we have upcoming events that we fear, we imagine them. And we get stuck in our minds in the middle of the event, picturing all the possible disasters. For example, our inability to talk, everything going wrong. We project disaster after disaster into it, ensuring, if not its failure, then our personal torture as we approach it.

The solution is straightforward. Instead of visualising the event itself, see yourself at the end of it. See yourself leaving it, and everyone involved feeling okay. The event has passed.

When we do that, the fear disappears. We are free to do whatever we want to prepare for it without being paralysed by fear.

If the fear returns, it is because we have gone back into the event. Stop. Go beyond it again. Feel your togetherness. It does not matter if you get the result you want or not.

Perhaps you are not meant to get it. Who can tell? Certainly not us.

There is no real ending. It's just the place where you stop the story.

Frank Herbert

Self-love

Every one of us needs to show how much we care for each other and, in the process, care for ourselves.

Diana, Princess of Wales

Low self-esteem is like driving through life with the hand brake on.

Maxwell Maltz

Positioning oneself in the perfect place, looking fabulous and taking a selfie is not self-love.

Self-love is being at peace with oneself, physically, mentally and spiritually accepting who we are.

Self-love and self-forgiveness go hand in hand.

Forgiving others is essential if we are to forgive ourselves.

We cannot love ourselves if we are dragging a cart full of negative emotions aimed at others and ourself. Self-love is treating the world and ourselves with acceptance, kindness and love. It is freedom.

True friends don't come with conditions.

Aaron Lauritsen

If you don't love yourself, nobody will. Not only that, you won't be good at loving anyone else. Loving starts with the self.

Wayne Dyer

Beginning

You only grow by coming to the end of something and by beginning something else.

John Irving

Our whole life has been an ongoing series of beginnings and endings.

How can it be that we haven't noticed that? Why do we leap into fear whenever we look into the future? Even the things we have done often can give us minor worry tweaks if we allow them to.

Oh, the fear of the unknown!

And yet everything that has happened to us has been a series of endings and beginnings. And hey, we are still here. At least we were the last time we looked. And even the most dreadful end or terrifying beginning didn't kill us, right?

So what's the big deal? Get a grip. Get on with it. Have courage. Hand the outcome over to your higher power or your heart and move through it with confidence because it isn't all up to you. And it will pass. It will just be a memory. Relax. Allow yourself to relax. And even if the worst happens, it won't be the worst. I can promise you that. The worst does not exist. It's just a figment in your mind.

Everything will be okay in the end. If it's not okay, it's not the end.

John Lennon

Goals

If you want to live a happy life, tie it to a goal, not to people or things.

Albert Einstein

Where do you spend most of your time if you are not in the present?

And I don't mean your worry times. Let's give them a rest. I mean your happy and exciting times.

Do you spend it in the past, reliving fantastic joy-filled events or envisioning the brilliant magical times you are moving towards in the future?

Maybe you do neither. Perhaps you have shut down all hope of happiness. Bah!

Humans are goal-seeking animals. If we do not have plans, we start to wither and die. If we dwell in the past, we renounce our right to live. If our thoughts about the future are dark, fear-filled horrors, then that is what we'll get. We want to choose something good in the future that we can move towards and do all we can to enhance it in our minds. Take steps towards making it a reality. That will keep us alive.

Oh, and as we get close to it happening, we want to start focusing on something beyond it. Don't let your life stop when you get there.

If you were born without wings, do nothing to prevent them from growing.

Coco Chanel

Living

Better to die fighting for freedom than be a prisoner all the days of your life.

Bob Marley

Are you living the life you want? Are the people and your daily activities the ones you want?

If your answer is not a resounding "Yes", perhaps this is an opportunity to consider it.

The things we do, think, express, and dwell on, create our reality and impact our world.

So if we give love rather than anger, disappointment, criticism, controlling thoughts, words, or actions, things will be better.

We will become whole, more complete, and stronger.

If we want to change, leave, or alter any area of our life or relationships, it will be easier when we approach it with inner strength.

Expose yourself to your deepest fear, after that, fear has no power, and fear of freedom shrinks and vanishes. You are free.

Jim Morrison

Now that she had nothing to lose, she was free.

Paulo Coelho

May 13

Help

We can't help everyone, but everyone can help someone.

Ronald Reagan

Are you helping anyone?
Can you help someone else as well?

I have found that if you love life, life will love you back.

Arthur Rubinstein

Prayer

God bless you, everyone.

Tiny Tim – Charles Dickens

I pray for people. I pray for an atheist. I asked him if he minded. He said, "No," he thought it was great that anybody would be thinking positively about him.

I talked to my sister about prayer because we had a mutual friend who was very ill. She said, "You must think that your prayers work then." "Yes," I replied straight away without a thought.

So my belief is that prayers work. I can send people love, healing and peace. Sometimes they go and die anyway, but that does not mean that prayers do not work.

We are, after all, spirits in a human body, waiting to move on again from the restriction that the human body imposes on us. So moving on is a relief when our time comes.

Do not stand at my grave and cry. I am not there; I did not die.

Clare Harner

Fear

Nothing in life is to be feared.

Marie Curie

What do you fear? What are your fears? What insanities tiptoe into your night and destroy your sleep?

What do you do about them?

Often if we do nothing, they are just stored beside the last one. The new fear arrives, blowing its whistle and banging its drums.

Do you tell anyone about your fears?

Telling others disempowers the fear.

Fear likes to have you all alone where it can do its damage, completely unchecked.

Fears come from the past or the future. They do not exist in the present second. Focus on your breathing, your body, and the things you can feel, touch, see, smell, and hear now.

Keep them all in your mind at the same time. The breath coming in through your nose, your arms touching, a sound in the room, the light on the ceiling, your chest rising and falling, your foot. Add your own.

Be aware.

Be present.

Be at peace.

Let us not look back in anger, nor forward in fear, but around in awareness.

James Thurber

Challenge

What does not kill me makes me stronger.

Friedrich Nietzsche

However bad what you are going through is, it will pass.

And, when we gaze back over our life, it is the worst moments that are often the most memorable, and in some ways, we can look back at them with a feeling of pride at our ability to have soldiered through them.

Of course, when we are really in it, drowning in our suffering, it is difficult to think about anything else. There appears to be no way out. We are doomed.

However, if we can lift our head just a tiny bit and remember that moment in the past, we survived! If we can do that. Then the present struggle diminishes. Even if only a little.

There are millions of people whose situation is worse than ours.

Courage is one step ahead of fear.

Coleman Young

If you're going through hell, keep going.

Winston Churchill

Scent

It's the closest thing we poor creatures have to magic, my dear – the ability to be transported through time by a waft of scent that unlocks a memory.

Jason Fry

I have a fruit bowl close by with, amongst other things, peaches.

Every so often, their scent envelopes me. It always surprises me when I am unexpectedly transported to a different world.

The best gardens are ones with hidden scents so that you walk around the corner into a cloud of scent.

Delight after delight.

If we have beautiful flowers without any smell, we miss out on a whole area of joy.

Fill your life with unique aromas and with magical delight.

Perfume is the scent that pours out of a flower's soul when crushed.

Matshona Dhliwayo

The scent of rain on a sultry spring evening is always an indulgence.

Kim Pape

May 18

Desires

*Do not spoil what you have by desiring what you have not,
remember that what you now have was once among the
things you only hoped for.*

Epicurus

Think for a moment of the goals, the things you have
wanted to possess in the past.

They may have given you a momentary buzz or high
(though often they didn't even do that), but now they are of
very little importance to you.

Desiring things in our life causes us stress and anxiety
and often disappointment. So it is worth considering what
you currently crave and decide whether it is worth the
emotional price demanded.

If you let go of the strife, and instead trust that whatever
you are meant to have will come, all the negative drains
disappear.

You are likely to achieve far more because you are not
blinding yourself with desire.

Take a breath.

Hand it over.

Let go.

Enjoy your life.

Help others to enjoy theirs.

You will be rewarded.

You <u>will</u> be rewarded.

You <u>will</u> be.

Ultimately, it is the desire, not the desired, that we love.

Friedrich Nietzsche

Handing Over

Rock bottom became the solid foundation on which I rebuilt my life.

J. K. Rowling

First you take a drink, then the drink takes a drink, then the drink takes you.

F. Scott Fitzgerald

I was walking down the Vegas Strip a little while ago – you know how one does – close to Caesar's Palace, and a man crossed the road towards me with what appeared to be an enormous roll of raw pizza dough hanging over his belt and halfway down to his crotch.

I just mention this because it is so easy to fill oneself with disgust and judgement.

If I were a gambling man, I'd make a reasonable wager that when he was a young lad, he didn't think, "When I'm grown up, I want to be able to walk down the Vegas Strip with my belly hanging over my jeans."

No. And if he had a choice, he would not be doing it now. No more than the alcoholic or drug addict would be drinking or drugging.

It is possible to change. To give up addictions. But it's impossible to do until we are ready. It isn't possible to do it alone. If we could do it alone, we would have done it already. Addicts give up endlessly, every day, even several times an hour, but to no avail.

We want to find people with whom we can share.

We want to find a power, and that power is not ourself, and say to the power "I can't do it. You do it."

Not easy. Not impossible.

Recovery is an acceptance that your life is in shambles, and you have to change it.

Jamie Lee Curtis

Change

The greatest discovery of all time is that a person can change his future by merely changing his attitude.

Oprah Winfrey

If you feel less than perfect, please do this now. If you feel serene, at peace and full of joy, please do it the next time you are troubled.

Okay, stand up.

Look above your head.

There is an opening about a yard wide, and all the shit is falling through it, onto you. Making you feel bad.

Okay, now take a step sideways, so you're no longer standing under the hole. The hole is still there, all its shit still pouring down, but you are no longer being covered in it.

You feel different, don't you?

Your shoulders feel different.

There may even be a trace of a smile on your face.

If you aren't sure about this, step back under the hole and feel the ghastliness.

I recommend that you step aside again.

Now whenever you are struggling or in a difficult situation, you can step sideways with a smile into the clean air. You can do this when you are with other people.

Enjoy.

True life is lived when tiny changes occur.

Leo Tolstoy

God

Would you think it odd if Hafiz said,
I am in love with every church
And Mosque
And temple
And any shrine
Because I know it is there
That people say the different names
Of the One God.

Hafiz

There is only one God, and it is always the same God.

This opens the door to the possibility of being in a position to let God into our lives.

God will meet you where you are in order to take you where he wants you to go.

Tony Evans

Learning

A teacher affects eternity, he can never tell where his influence stops.

Henry Adams

Sometimes it feels as if we are under a barrage of attack from everyone. Everyone shouting and demanding our attention. Sometimes, the reverse appears true, and we are being ignored and disregarded.

The trick is, no, it isn't a trick. The solution is to remember that everyone we are with, and every situation we are in, are all here to teach us something.

We may well not want to learn what we are being offered. The very idea that there is some purpose to what is going on may be abhorrent to us, but that's okay.

If we need to learn something, the lesson will be repeated until we know it.

The moment we step away from whatever is going on and view it as a lesson, it changes.

It's our choice. We don't have to view it like that. We can just go on having a difficult time for as long as we like. The decision is ours.

Never stop learning. If you have a teacher, you never stop being a student.

Elizabeth Rohan

Honesty

Honesty is often very hard. The truth is often painful. But the freedom it can bring is worth the trying.

Fred Rogers

I was in a food supermarket the other day, and the boy stacking the shelves had such foul body odour that it nearly made me stumble.

What does one do in a situation like that? What is the correct thing to do? Nothing? Pretend that one is not overwhelmed by his scent?

Or does one say, "Excuse me, but your body odour is unacceptable?"

Of course, tradition has it that one does nothing. But is that right?

And are we to assume that he has no idea that he stinks? Surely he must know. Maybe he has a 'condition' that he can do nothing about?

It makes one think, though. I am afraid that, on this occasion, I did nothing.

Now I believe I should have said something. So I hope that when I am unfortunate enough to encounter someone like that again, I will have the courage to speak.

And what, I wonder, will you do?

Honesty and frankness make you vulnerable. Be honest and frank anyway.

Kent M. Keith

Freedom

When I discover who I am, I'll be free.

Ralph Ellison

Stop for a moment.

Imagine the part of you that holds you back, no longer exists.

That you are free... to be yourself without restraint.

The place to start is within ourselves. Genuine unconditional love for ourselves.

Stop for a moment, and feel total unconditional love for yourself now.

It feels different.

We go through our lives constantly putting the brakes on, achieving less than we could. Not quite daring to share our love with others. Or perhaps even worse, using love to enslave or control others.

If we are to have freedom, we have to give freedom to others. If we want to achieve this, we want to replace our negative thoughts, judgements, and control with love.

If you can love yourself and all your flaws, you can love other people so much better. And that makes you so happy.

Kristin Chenoweth

Letting Go

If you truly want to be respected by people you love, you must prove to them that you can survive without them.

Michael Bassey Johnson

Letting go of people, places, and things can be hard. Things keep reminding us. We have another little (or large) stab to our heart. The raw emotion floods through us. And sometimes, even years later, after we have completely moved on, we see, hear, or smell something, and everything comes flooding back.

All of which is called being human.

And although it may not feel like it when we are suffering, we do have a choice

We choose the memory we focus on. We can go into the pain and increase that, or we can take a moment and be calm.

If we love someone and are not with them, we can give them the freedom to be. If we truly, love them, we want them to be happy even if we are not with them.

If we think of them with anger and hatred, we are the person we are hurting.

Pull down a screen between you and them. Let them exist behind it, and learn to exist, in the world, on your side of the screen, without bitterness or sorrow.

Choose peace. Even if you only get a second of peace, that is more than you had. If you've done it once, you can do it again.

Go for two seconds. Surprise yourself.

Cry. Forgive. Learn. Move on. Let your tears water the seeds of your future happiness.

Steve Maraboli

Meditation

A sharp knife cuts the quickest and hurts the least.

Katharine Hepburn

Relax your shoulders.

There, that's better, isn't it?

I am sure that you have, at some time in your life, done the same task with a blunt and a sharp knife. The difference is extraordinary. Sharpness cuts a mass of time from the job.

And if you sharpen your own knives, you know the time it takes you to sharpen, and the time saved. Obvious, isn't it? One would be insane not to do it.

Relax your shoulders.

And you hadn't even noticed them tensing. I've said it before, people say, "I don't have time to meditate!" And even if they make time in the morning, for example, they then go through their day without having mini-meditations. So they leap from event to event carrying all the stresses and struggles from the last to the next.

Their knife is getting blunt, but they don't notice.

Relax your shoulders.

See how easy it is to tense them.

Meditation, mini-meditations, and a slow conscious breath are all ways to clear your head.

Sharpen your knife, and find an elegance in the way you do things.

A knife is only as good as the one who wields it.

Patrick Ness

Relationships

I mean, if the relationship can't survive the long term, why on earth would it be worth my time and energy for the short term.

Nicholas Sparks

I had a friend who worked in Saudi Arabia when I was in my twenties. He would return to the UK a couple of times a year, and we always met and spent time together. After about eight years, he moved back to the UK, and we only met every couple of years. Because we were living in the same place, it appeared that we didn't need to meet.

When people fall in love and are dating but not living together, they tend to spend every second they can on the phone or together, constantly doing things with or for each other.

When they move in together, they take each other for granted. They do things separately. Their consideration for each other nearly always diminishes.

When one person in a relationship retires and is around all the time, their relationship can suddenly become a nightmare.

So. Does this ring any bells? If so, are you going to do anything about it?

It is almost certainly worth it if you want true joy in your life.

When you stop expecting people to be perfect, you can like them for who they are.

Donald Miller

Things change. And friends leave. And life doesn't stop for anybody.

Stephen Chbosky

Change

The snake which cannot cast its skin has to die. As well the minds which are prevented from changing their opinions; they cease to mind.

Friedrich Nietzsche

When confronted with a difficulty, challenge, pain-filled experience, or any negative in our life, our natural reaction is to dive more deeply into it. Creating suffering in our mind and body.

The truth is that hidden within every trouble, there is a treasure. It is waiting for us to find it and crack it open.

It may seem inconceivable that there can be a treasure in the awfulness we are being swept along in.

But there is a treasure.

And as soon as we realise it and accept that, the difficulties we are faced with change.

We have been through challenging times in our life, and are still here.

It is by going down into the abyss that we recover the treasures of life. Where you stumble, there lies your treasure.

Joseph Campbell

Blame

When you blame and criticise others, you are avoiding some truth about yourself.

Deepak Chopra

We are, by nature, blamers. As infants, we tried to make sense of the world, and when things did not go how we wanted, we tried to understand why we were not getting what we wanted. And so, we realised that it was "their fault". They were not doing what was needed.

Unless we have done an immense amount of work on ourselves, this is still our default setting.

It is no longer as bad as it was – we discovered that people didn't like us if we behaved too badly, so we made adjustments. But often, when something goes "wrong", we look for something other than ourselves to blame.

Most of us will not completely give up blaming. But we can reduce the number of times we damage ourselves and others by blaming .

Go on. Be brave. Accept and own responsibility. Life is better that way.

Would you like yourself, if you met yourself?

Amit Kalantri

May 30

Acceptance

You can't run away from yourself.

Bob Marley

You can always improve your situation. But you do so by facing it, not by running away.

Brad Warner

You and I both know this. We cannot run away. There is no place where we might go where we are not.

A new lover, car, location, or job are not the solution because we are there too.

When we have internal struggles and unhappiness, we want to address them, or nothing will change.

And we want to discuss them with somebody, honestly, otherwise, they are secrets, and secrets destroy us. The good news is that our struggle is a stepping stone to new freedom. Once we confront it, deal with it and learn from it.

Realising that we can look at our current pain with gratitude changes it. It disarms it. We are already moving through it.

For after all, the best thing one can do when it is raining is let it rain.

Henry Wadsworth Longfellow

Death

Death is not the greatest loss in life. The greatest loss is what dies inside us while we live.

Norman Cousins

I used to be terrified of dying, yet I did not want to live.
Now I do not fear death, but I do not want to die.
So what happened?

Before, I wanted to be in charge of my life. I thought I knew how things should be done. Or I just let go of it all and let it fall apart. I was a mess.

And now? I haven't "found God". I've met people who have found God, and always found them difficult to understand.

I have discovered how to meditate and go inside, to find answers from my heart rather than from my head.

There's a saying, "Let go and let God". When I decide to let go, I say, "Okay, I don't know what to do or what the answer is." I can then accept whatever is going to happen without a fight.

It feels as if I've let a very heavy overcoat slip off my shoulders. I am liberated. Light. Able to move forward without fear.

Some of us think holding on makes us strong, but sometimes it is letting go.

Hermann Hesse

I am

responsible

June 1

Writing

You do not need to leave your room. Remain sitting at your table and listen. Do not even listen, simply wait, be quiet, still and solitary. The world will freely offer itself to you to be unmasked, it has no choice, it will roll in ecstasy at your feet.

Franz Kafka

This is what happens to me when I sit down to write. It pours from me across the page. I am truly blessed.

It is the stillness and the quiet. It is taking a seed and letting it perform its magic.

It happens to me when I am with others, when I stop all the me, me, me shouting in my head and relax and give my attention and love to them.

Einstein said that all his significant ideas came to him when he daydreamed. We have so much more in us than we can imagine if we can learn to stop and allow it to unfold.

If my doctor told me I had only six minutes to live, I wouldn't brood. I'd type a little faster.

Isaac Asimov

Creativity doesn't wait for that perfect moment. It fashions its own perfect moments out of ordinary ones.

Bruce Garrabrandt

Simplifying

*Sometimes surrender means giving up trying to
understand and becoming comfortable with not knowing.*

Eckhart Tolle

Oh, the turmoil. The constant struggle as we try to
unravel everything in our lives.

We are juggling our relationships with our children,
partners, jobs and all our perceived shortcomings that erupt
in our minds, like a box of fireworks that have all
accidentally exploded simultaneously.

What is the solution?

Sorry, you didn't hear my question.

WHAT IS THE SOLUTION?

One thing is for sure, the questions, all lumped together,
are far too big for anyone to untangle. We cannot deal with
them all at once.

So the answer has to be to take a deep breath, go inside,
and allow them to settle. Then accept there is probably no
solution to many of our troubles, so let them go. If there is
nothing we can do about it, accept that. Be peaceful, knowing
that you do not need to solve it.

And if you can pick one thing you might be able to
improve, choose that. Just focus on that. Give yourself a
break.

*The shorter way to do many things is to only do one thing
at a time.*

Mozart

June 3

Communication

Communication is a skill you can learn. It's like riding a bicycle or typing. If you're willing to work at it, you can rapidly improve the quality of every part of your life.

Brian Tracy

When we are with children, we can get down to their level, participate, and make suggestions that they will (probably) happily go along with.

Or we can stay up here and bark orders at them, which they may (unwillingly) obey. And even if they obey, you can surely see that this has not improved your relationship with them.

Which of these two people do you think they want to be around more, and whom do they respect and love the more? Which are you training them to become, the well-rounded adventurer or the angry disciplinarian?

And here's a thought. Most people treat other people the same way they treat their children, and they disguise their behaviours slightly to make them more acceptable in the adult world.

The single biggest problem in communication is the illusion that it has taken place.

George Bernard Shaw

June 4

Judgement

Even God doesn't propose to judge a man till his last days,
why should you and I?

Dale Carnegie

See yourself in others.

When you are with others, rather than judging, labelling or looking down upon or up at them, you can see yourself in them instead.

They and you are one.

We forget that (if indeed we ever knew it).

Our natural response to being with anyone is to make judgements about them in one way or another, and that creates blocks between us. Blocks that we are creating.

If instead, we see them as ourselves, and accept their being and our being as one, the blocks dissolve. We will experience our time with them in a completely new light.

Of course, we have to decide to do it first. And to continue to do it. And to do it again.

Which, at first, will seem like an almost impossible effort. But persevere. The rewards are incredible.

Standing each by his monster, they looked at each other,
and smiled.

E. M. Forster

Handing Over

You must be the person you have never had the courage to be. Gradually, you will discover that you are that person, but until you can see this clearly, you must pretend and invent.

Paulo Coelho

Fake it till you make it.

Act as if... you can do it.

Even if you don't believe you know how to.

Have faith.

Faith that it will work out.

Faith that you do not need to be in control, doing, doing, doing.

Accept what happens.

Hand it over.

Even if you have no idea what you are handing it over to.

Learn to say, "This is too big for me. I cannot do it alone. You do it. You make the decisions. You lead me. I trust you. I believe that it will all work out if you are in control."

You can start the next thing without fear when you do that because you have faith.

It is in your hands to create a better world for all who live in it.

Nelson Mandela

June 6

Breathing

Learn how to exhale, the inhale will take care of itself.

Carla Melucci Ardito

Have you ever noticed that your body changes, softens, and relaxes when you breathe out?

It has a vulnerability.

It is open.

If you breathe out and pause, there is time to consider what is going on.

You think differently, calmly. It's an excellent place to come to decisions or allow ideas in.

When we breathe in, we are, by comparison, in fight mode. We are in power mode.

Our thinking is different. Our default setting is the in-breath, and the out-breath mode never gets a look into the situation, which is a great shame because we are so much more than just the in-breath.

Breathe. Let go. And remind yourself that this very moment is the only one you truly know you have for sure.

Oprah Winfrey

June 7

Pain

One thing you can't hide is when you're crippled inside.

John Lennon

Turn your wounds to wisdom.

Oprah Winfrey

Bring on the pain.
If that is what it takes, bring it on.
Drown me with pain.
Drown me.
Give me more. Please. Please. Please!

I know that I will not change until the pain is immense enough. I know it. So please increase it as quickly as possible.

Here I am. At this moment, I am suffering so much. It is unbearable. But not intolerable enough. Not so indescribably awful that I will change. No. No. No. I'll wallow in this because, I know that I am alive when I do. The pain, the awfulness, proves it.

And there is one truth that I know absolutely. Other people discarded their pain long before it got as bad as mine. So I know that I don't need to go on fighting it. I am fighting and clinging to it at the same time.

All I have to do to stop and surrender. Surrender to the peace that lives within me. Surrender to the friend that is here to help me, who cannot help me until I surrender. As long as I am fighting, the wall is too thick for anything to penetrate.

One word frees us of all the weight and pain of life:
That word is love.

Sophocles

June 8

Senses

I go to nature to be soothed and healed, and to have my senses put in order.

John Burroughs

Do me a favour.

Get a piece of fruit. If it has been in the fridge, let it warm up.

Hold it in your hand, touch and feel it.

Now breathe it in. Slowly.

Think about it with your nose.

Look at it. Rotate it. Really look at it. You have almost certainly never really studied it.

Now bite it and explore the chewed piece in your mouth. Envelop yourself in the flavour.

Now bite it again. Once. Twice. Slowly feel it as it spreads over your tongue. And very slowly chew it up and allow it to disappear down your throat.

Repeat.

Often.

Slowly.

Remember slowly.

Lose your mind and come to your senses.

Fritz Perls

June 9

Meditation

Nature does not hurry, yet everything is accomplished.

Lao Tzu

Meditation. A gateway to peace.

If we do not meditate when things are good, we certainly won't when things are bad.

Just a few minutes a day. I use an app called Insight Timer, which is excellent. But there are many others. I meditate with it every morning for a few minutes, and I listen to another as I go to sleep.

If I have any particular challenge, I find specific meditations.

But most importantly, throughout the day, I take a deep conscious breath, hold it in, and let it slowly out. This changes everything. You cannot think of anything else when you take a conscious breath. You can do it in a room full of people without them knowing. Don't get washed away in the storms of life.

Do it.

So powerful.

Feelings come and go like clouds in a windy sky. Conscious breathing is my anchor.

Thich Nhat Hanh

Wind chimes

The sound of hope,
Is just like a shining wind chime,
It's low,
It's mysterious,
It's weirdly comforting,
It's something for nothing.

Harshna Handoo

Wind chimes out of doors are a nuisance. They make too much noise when the wind blows. Why would anyone add unnecessary noise that they have no control over in their life?

Wind chimes indoors are lovely. I have (only) three in my house. The best, loudest and most musical hangs in the centre of my kitchen, so as I walk past and brush the disc below it, it rings out.

It is such a joy. Especially as it was given to me by someone I love, I recommend that you get some dotted around your home. Listen to them carefully before you buy them to make sure the sound they make is a sound you like.

I think I will do nothing for a long time but listen
And accrue what I hear into myself...
and let sounds contribute towards me.

Walt Whitman

June 11

Overwhelm

Some days, you will feel like the ocean. Some days, you will feel like you are drowning in it.

Lora Mathis

We all know that a journey starts with a single step. You write a novel one word at a time. And yet, by and large, we forget that this applies to everything in our lives.

We slump in our chairs and think that we can't. We don't know how to make any changes in our lives. And that is because the moment we think about what we want to alter, we look at a completed chapter or the ten-thousandth step of the journey. It is overwhelming. We give up before we start.

Pull it back. Pull it back. Right back to the first tiny action and commit to that. And then pull it back again, stop running ahead of yourself, and commit to the second little action.

BUT NOT BEFORE YOU HAVE FINISHED THE FIRST.

Go on. Surprise yourself. Enjoy.

Every word has consequences. Every silence, too.

Jean-Paul Sartre

Release

We cannot sow seeds with clenched fists. To sow, we must open our hands.

Adolfo Perez Esquivel

At times in our lives, we are closed up. Everything locked away and full of suffering. Suffering for us and at least disquieting for others.

A good question to ask at such times is, why? Why are we being so self-indulgent? Yes, there may be a million reasons that have to do with "them" or "it", but we know that none of these are real.

Yes, they may have done unspeakable things. Yes, what they've done may affect us now. They burnt our house down, and we had nowhere to live. But the cause, the house burning, happened then, and as long as we carry the grievance, we suffer.

They are mistreating us now, at this minute, but we are consenting by being here. Yes, leaving can be terrifying, but we allow it to happen if we stay.

Why?

Fighting back is just another way to continue it.

We may not think or believe it, but we are free. We can choose what we do and where we do it. If we don't exercise our right to do this, the blame is ours.

Oh my god! Did I write that!

Everyone's chest is a living room wall with awkwardly placed photographs hiding fist-shaped holes.

Andrea Gibson

Perspective

When you really listen to another person from their point of view, and reflect back to them that understanding, it's like giving them emotional oxygen.

Stephen Covey

So often, when we are talking with others, that is what we do, talk.

Yes, we are sharing the depth of our extensive knowledge with them, and yes, we are, hopefully, trying to be helpful.

And we may be incredibly useful to them.

But here's a thought, here's something that we can do, which often makes a vast difference to what we say and how useful it is.

Take a moment and change places with them as completely as possible. Experience what they are feeling and thinking. Look at it through their eyes. And then later, speak.

What you say will be different.

It is also beneficial to do this if we are ever in disagreement with someone. Looking at and understanding the situation from their point of view will change everything.

I have wanted you to see out of my eyes so many times.

Elizabeth Berg

Openness

*Until the mind is open, the heart stays closed. The open
mind is the key to the open heart.*

Byron Katie

Sometimes, as I sit at my table to write, my dog comes
over and, uninvited launches herself onto my lap.

I wonder why as I stroke her and whisper in her ear.

What is it that makes her do that?

I am in tune. I am one. I am God. It is because I do not
really write. I read the words back as they appear on the
page.

During these gentle minutes, I open myself and my dog
wants to be embraced by that.

I know an incredible peace and ease when I write. A gift.
So much greater than I am.

*Openness of mind strengthens the truth in us and removes
the dross from it, if there is any.*

Mahatma Gandhi

June 15

Control

*Life will give you whatever experience is the most helpful
for the evolution of your consciousness. How do you know
this is the experience you need? Because this is the
experience you are having at the moment.*

Eckhart Tolle

At the moment, today, because I am ill, people have taken
control of my life. There are things that they won't let me do.
"No," they say, "You keep out the way. We are doing
everything now!"

I know that I shall become involved again. But not for a
while.

It is tough for me to let go. To allow this to happen. No,
not tough, really, really challenging.

But I guess it must be good for me too. It is what I need to
learn today. And so, I am learning with a smile.

I've nipped in here secretly to write this. No telling on me,
Okay!

*To keep your secret is wisdom, but to expect others to keep
it is folly.*

Samuel Johnson

Nothing makes us so lonely as our secrets.

Paul Tournier

June 16

Wrong

Being wrong is acceptable, but staying wrong is totally unacceptable.

Jack D. Schwager

You are wrong. Nearly everything you believe in is wrong.

And the more intensely you believe in it, the more likely it is that you are wrong.

Nearly everything that most of us do is driven by our ego. It is caused by a mixture of self-interest and a need to keep us locked into the behaviours that we mistakenly believe serve us best.

We do things, say things, and feel things, to prove that we are okay and are as good as, if not better than others.

And it is all a lie.

We are only here to share love and peace.

We know this is the truth at the core of our being.

A long habit of not thinking a thing wrong gives it a superficial appearance of being right.

Thomas Paine

Acceptance

If we will imagine the thing we want and do our part to "be in the right place at the right time", there isn't anything we can't do, be, or attain.

Daniel Willey

Let's stop for a little.

Let's settle back.

And now, please, let us assume, no, let us know, that we are in the right place at this moment in time. Every action we have taken or not taken has led us to this very second.

Accept with your whole being that you are in the right place. Accept and know it.

It simplifies everything. All our troubles, past and future, dissolve. They are no longer relevant. There is now and we are here. Exactly where we are meant to be. And that will still be true in a few hours as we deal with whatever is happening.

It empowers us. It releases us. We can live unfettered.

We must let go of the life we have planned so as to accept the one that is waiting for us.

Joseph Campbell

June 18

Reacting

We often add to our pain and suffering by being overly sensitive, over-reacting to minor things, and sometimes taking things too personally.

Dalai Lama

For some of us, over reacting is almost an illness. We leap down their throat before they've even taken a breath. Many of us occasionally act without any real thought.

While others seem to glide along, apparently untroubled by the disasters surrounding them.

How on earth do they do that? How can they remain calm in the face of such strife?

I believe the answer is they are not mechanically trying to control their life or anyone else's. They have learnt to let go. They understand at a deep level that what is happening will run its course. And they are okay with that.

They have also discovered that they will get far more joy from being at peace than from being right. So they no longer try to impose their rightness on the situation.

The life of inner peace, being harmonious and without stress, is the easiest type of existence.

Norman Vincent Peale

June 19

Ego

*The moment you become aware of the ego in you, it is
strictly speaking no longer the ego, but just an old,
conditioned mind-pattern. Ego implies unawareness.
Awareness and ego cannot co-exist.*

Eckhart Tolle

So here we are again, battling with the ego. (Oh by the
way, have you read the Power of Now by Eckhart Tolle. It
would be a mistake not to.)

So yes, the ego, the madman who inhabits our minds,
screaming insanities at us. When we stop, step back and look
at the ego and the nonsense it is spouting, we disempower it.

The ego is like a child at a birthday party, overdosing on
sugar and running uncontrollably around. When we realise
that, plop him down on our knee, smooth his hair, and he
may fall asleep.

We can lead our lives with serenity and love that lives in
our hearts. It is always there, waiting for us to call on it,
though the ego often drowns out the voice of calm, and love.

*Part of me suspects that I am a loser, and the other part of
me thinks I'm God Almighty.*

John Lennon

Enlightenment is ego's ultimate disappointment.

Chogyam Trungpa

Problems

I don't want to be a genius – I have enough problems just trying to be a man.

Albert Camus

A mistake repeated more than once is a decision.

Paulo Coelho

Are you part of the problem or part of the solution?

I had a sales manager once who, when people came and dumped their problems on him, would take them out to the dustbins, where he'd tell them to leave all their rubbish and only come and see him when they were part of the solution.

If you feel sorry for yourself, hard done by, unappreciated, or disrespected, you are part of the problem.

If they are the cause of your problem or are doing it to you, you are part of the problem. If they won't do what you want, you are part of the problem. And "spoiler alert", the fact that you feel this way about them will not change them.

There is only one place where you can make a change, and that is within you.

When you go to anyone and complain about anything, you disrespect the listener. You have just turned up with a vast vat of shit, which you've jumped into and are now frantically and ineffectually stirring round and round.

So please, before you go and tell them your woes, look carefully at what you are going to say and edit out all the unnecessary moans and gripes. Think about what you could do to improve the situation, and discuss that with them.

Make it a habit.

You fix what you can fix and you let the rest go. If there ain't nothin' to be done about it, it ain't even a problem. It's just an aggravation.

Cormac McCarthy

Self-defence

Self-defence is not just a set of techniques; it's a state of mind, and it begins with the belief that you are worth defending.

Rorion Gracie

Some people are constantly on the lookout for others taking advantage of them, putting them down, or disrespecting them. All their senses are on high alert. If someone merely brushes past, they react as if they are being attacked. They are constantly on guard against the world, with more sensitivity in some areas than others. Greater expectations of attack from one group while almost too much at ease with another.

If we are on guard a lot of the time, we cannot be happy. We cannot have peace.

Peace is really good. I know. I have peace nearly all the time. If I can, then you can too, I recommend it.

Look at your battles. If you are honest, you will find that most of them are unimportant. Discard them. They are simply your ego pressing your "let's feel like shit again" button.

And the two or three that are real? Address them. Talk to the people involved. Do not rage away in silence. Silence is a killer. We can only disarm things by talking about them.

Initially, speak to a third party and get clarity about it, then talk to the person who is offending you, but do it without hostility or blame. Explain why it is not working. If they are someone you want in your life, they will meet you and change. You do not want them in your life if they will not.

A tree never hits an automobile, except in self-defence.

Woody Allen

June 22

Leaf

*The leaves spring green tips floated by, caressing softly
countless gentle beings.*

Jazz Feylynn

Outside my window, there are a few million leaves.
Incredible. Individual.

Ask most people to paint a tree, and they pick a green and
spread it across the page.

But look. No leaf is the same colour all over. It is such a
vibrant mass of colours, exploding into the day.

I go into the elegance of my heart, I sit and lose myself in
a square meter (or less) of leaves, and I simply absorb. I am
filled with such a wealth of peace and joy.

I breathe in the world.

I think it.

I feel so blessed.

Even a leaf in the wind settles sometimes.

Alison Goodman

Learning

Life is a succession of lessons which must be lived to be understood. All is riddle, and the key to a riddle is another riddle.

Ralph Waldo Emerson

Life is a classroom.

We are put here to learn. The people we meet are here to teach us what we need to discover.

If we do not learn our lessons from one person, we will be sent another and another until we learn. And so, it makes sense to consider what it might be that we are supposed to be learning from the current set of circumstances we are in.

Do we need to "take things less seriously", "be more patient", "have quiet times", "be more attentive and giving?"

You can think about what your lesson might be. The list is endless.

But if we realise that every time I meet "them", it makes me feel "X". I can delve into what the message within "X" is, learn, and start to move on.

Life is about accepting the challenges along the way, choosing to keep moving forward, and savouring the journey.

Roy T. Bennett

June 24

Never

Do not take life too seriously. You will never get out of it alive.

Elbert Hubbard

Never is a big word.

It lessens us. It slams doors, blindly.

It limits our thinking.

"Never again", after a less good or even a bad experience, assumes that all future events will be as bad or worse.

We fill ourselves with resistance or negative expectations.

But life changes. We change. When we are open to life, it is better and fuller.

We may not get what we want, but we will nearly always get what we expect.

So why choose to expect something bad? That would certainly be weird.

A person who never made a mistake never tried anything new.

Albert Einstein

It is not death that man should fear, but he should fear never beginning to live.

Marcus Aurelius

Respect

Everyone in society should be a role model, not only for their own self-respect, but for respect from others.

Barry Bonds

We are not objects. We move through our lives, unique and magnificent. We are alive. We deserve respect, and we want to treat everyone we come into contact with, with respect. How can we expect it from others if we are not doing it?

So often, groups of people are lumped together and collectively disrespected. Men do it to women. And women do it to men. Parents do it to their children. One country to another country. One religion to another.

The list goes on.

If you are not doing it in some area of your life, then you are an exception. Bravo!

We are all precious, unique, incredible beings doing the best we can. Let us look for and find the good. Let us be the good.

I'm not concerned with your liking or disliking me... All I ask is that you respect me as a human being.

Jackie Robinson

Doing

Don't let yesterday take up too much of today.

Will Rogers

Anything which you have in profusion is poison.

Amit Kalantri

Doing. Doing. Doing.

Endlessly doing. Planning the next doing to charge towards, while berating ourselves for our failures and shortcomings.

There is, as they say, "No rest for the wicked," and although we may not want to own up to it, a tiny part of us thinks we are wicked. Of course, we believe others can't see that because we keep it so well hidden. And actually, others probably don't process their knowledge because they couldn't care less, in all honesty.

And when we plop down and take the drug of TV, the computer game, housework, or whatever mind-altering medicine we use, some part of us is still doing, doing, doing, underneath. It is just that our doing of choice numbs enough so that we don't have the endless doing chatter.

All of that insanity is ego-driven. And yes, you may only have a mild case of it – most of the time. But it is there.

And we know how to stop it too. But we cannot be bothered. So much easier to pop another pill and dumb it down. But we have peace and love and serenity in our hearts. It is always there, and can be ours anytime we choose to access it.

Nothing can disturb your peace of mind unless you allow it to.

Roy T. Bennett

Distraction

People don't need to be scared. I tickle sharks. I do, when they swim by.

Michael Muller

You know, when you are sitting there, nothing has changed, and you start to get a tickle on your nose, about halfway up the right nostril. It starts small, almost unnoticeable. Maybe we get a little tickle on the top of our head whilst the nose develops. There it is now. Our hand starts to move up to scratch it. But no, we manage to stop it. But it's getting bigger and bigger, shouting out, scratch me, scratch me.

So let me ask you, what happened? What changed? What caused the tickle?

Sometimes there is a reason, something is touching your neck, and you have to scratch it. But wait a moment, wasn't it touching your neck for ages before it started to tickle?

You see, tickles are created by your mind, not your body. And that being the case, if you spend a few seconds identifying and mentally feeling different parts of your body, you can change it, so the tickle disappears.

It works on pain too. My son falls and hurts his knee, and I ask, "does your elbow hurt? How about the little finger on your left hand? How about your right foot, does that hurt? Are you sure it doesn't?"

After four to five body parts, he stops crying, and the pain in his knee has gone. I can do it to myself too. Why indulge in pain?

You can always find a distraction if you're looking for one.

Tom Kite

Feelings

Don't deny your feelings, they are who you are.

Father Patrick Cleary

We have feelings.

Just like that, "Bosh!" they are upon us.

Feelings of anger, joy, sadness, loneliness, superiority, and jealousy are just a few. They sweep through our body.

But here's the thing. We do not have to go into them. We do not have to let the anger, sadness, whatever, fill us and take us over.

If instead, we observe the feeling, look at it and register it. "I feel sad" or "I feel angry", etc. just note it but choose not to go into it. Choose not to be overwhelmed by the feeling.

Just let it go and move on with your day.

Enjoy.

Thoughts are the shadows of our feelings – always darker, emptier and simpler.

Friedrich Nietzsche

The closest to perfection a person ever comes, is when he fills out a job application.

Stanley Randall

Connectedness

And as we felt our own light shine, we unconsciously give other people permission to do the same. As we are liberated from our own fear, our presence automatically liberates others.

Marianne Williamson

Everything is connected.

What we give is what we get.

Yes, yes, I know, I know, you've heard that a million times. It's like "this too shall pass", one of those old chestnuts that people pop out of their mouths, and nobody processes.

Our actions and words set in motion a chain of events that circle back to us. If we are being kind, loving, generous, and thoughtful towards others, that is how we will be treated. Not necessarily by the people we treat well but by others, we meet as we go through our lives.

And you know this is true. You only have to remember the situation you went into bristling with anger and another that you went into feeling calm and loving to see the responses you got and how the situation developed. So decide to give the world love, compassion, and thoughtfulness.

Enjoy.

A human being is a part of the whole called by us Universe, a part limited in time and space. He experiences himself, his thoughts, and feelings as something separate from the rest, a kind of optical delusion of his consciousness. This delusion is a kind of prison for us, restricting us to our personal desires and to affection for a few persons nearest to us. Our task must be to free ourselves from this prison by widening our circle of compassion to embrace all living creatures and the whole of nature in its beauty.

Albert Einstein

June 30

Forgiveness

*He that cannot forgive others breaks the bridge over which
he must pass himself; for every man has need to be
forgiven.*

Thomas Fuller

Forgiveness is vital to our well-being.

Totally.

Because as long as we are judging others, our ego is controlling our thinking.

As long as we carry the hurts from the past, real or imagined, our egos are in charge.

We are impaling ourselves on a flaming blade of poison. When we start to view the world with love, everything changes.

Remember, or realise, we always see the world we choose to see.

*The bitterest of tears shed over graves are for words left
unsaid and deeds left undone.*

Harriet Beecher Stowe

Keep

it

simple

Rhythm

*In every change, in every falling leaf there is some pain,
some beauty. And that's the way new leaves grow.*

Amit Ray

It is the first of July, and the leaves have started to fall from the trees. My initial response is one of sadness. Sadness and amazement that they have begun to fall so early.

And yet.

I love the seasons. I feel so grateful to live in a place with four well-defined seasons. And I know that most of the leaves will hang on until October.

There is a rhythm to life. Birth, suffering, joy and death.

It is that simple. And when we allow ourselves to accept that, it makes everything so much easier. It removes a lot of our futile battles and suffering.

*The first step towards change is awareness. The second step
is acceptance.*

Nathaniel Brandon

July 2

Beliefs

To live is the rarest thing in the world. Most people exist,
that is all.

Oscar Wilde

Are you happy the way you are now?

Do you think that maybe some of your beliefs are holding
you back and causing you pain?

I am not going to tell you that you got it wrong, that you
made a mistake, or that your views are... incorrect?

No, I am not that foolish.

And I want you to go on liking me and being my friend.

However...

Is it a possibility?

I'm not asking you to say "yes" immediately if you don't
choose to.

But do you think life might be simpler if you didn't hold
onto your beliefs so tightly?

Suppose you have even the slightest glimmer of
acceptance of this idea. I suggest you discuss it peacefully
with someone you trust and see if it might be possible, with
fewer black and white certainties, to lead a more comfortable
life.

This is just an idea. It's not even as strong as throwing a
pebble into a pond. Instead, it's the vaguest thought about
how the water might look if a pebble were thrown into it.

A thing is not necessarily true because a man dies for it.

Oscar Wilde

Inner Being

*I believe that what people call God is something in all of us.
I believe that what Jesus and Mohammed and Buddha and
all the rest said was right. It's just the translations that have
gone wrong.*

John Lennon

May I offer you a different perspective, another way to view and interact with yourself? (If you do not like it, that is fine discard it, but please give it a chance first. It changes things.)

Can you start by assuming that your inner being, soul, and God are who you are? That is the real, the true you. You are pure light because you are your essence.

Now think for a moment of the you that is called whatever you are called. (Mary, John, Steff, whatever you call yourself.)

And then realise that all the fears, doubts, and emotions are in your body, not in the inner you.

Your inner voice can talk to you. "It's alright, Mary, there is nothing to fear. I am love. I love you. I am love. You are love."

Be still.

Be calm.

Let your inner being talk to you and guide you.

*The Lord created you and me for the purpose of becoming
Gods like himself.*

Brigham Young

Commitment

The level of success you achieve will be in direct proportion to the depth of your commitment.

Roy T. Bennett

Whatever we do, we want to do it. There is no point in half-heartedly trying to hit a ball because it is more likely to go in the wrong direction when we hit it.

So whatever we are doing now, in this instant (and the next instant, and the next, and the next, till the end of time), we want to put everything we have into it. And if we do not want to do it, we want to say, "No, I'm not going to do it". That is fine too, because that is committing oneself to it.

I know it's difficult. There are so many tedious little grey areas in your life, and it is much easier just to go along, go with the flow, and survive without thought. Of course, it is. But would you not like to feel empowered? Wouldn't you like to go to bed filled with gratitude towards yourself?

So, starting now, live fully, moment by moment. Be present, be the best you can be. And feel the difference as you go through your life.

Unless commitment is made, there are only promises and hopes, but no plans.

Peter F. Drucker

July 5

Moving On

My mother groan'd! My father wept. Into the dangerous world I leapt.

William Blake

There is no going back.

We journey on and through, changing and growing as we go.

The trauma we experienced during our birth, the inexplicable eviction from our wonderful, comfortable home into this world, is unbelievable. And yet, somehow, we survived.

And we can accept that there is no going back. No return.

And this is true of, will be true of, everything we go through. The sooner we can accept that the journey is inevitable, the easier it is to travel on and embrace rather than fight the changes we are offered.

Actually, I don't remember being born, it must have happened during one of my blackouts.

Jim Morrison

July 6

Hugging

He that plants trees loves others besides himself.

Thomas Fuller

I hugged my first tree today in the high street, which in retrospect, is probably not the best place for a virgin hugger. Though don't let that put you off. Next time, I think I shall find a tree in a forest or a wood.

So anyway, there I was, hugging. I have hugging friends who praise the practice enthusiastically, so I thought that I, as an adventurer, should give it a go.

My eyes were closed, but I was aware of the passers-by, I couldn't see them, but I knew they were there. My ego shouting, "They're all staring at you", and "Someone's going to come up to you in a minute and ask if you're alight."

I managed to push my ego aside and give myself to the hugging. After a while, wonderful peace. A different rhythm of peace than usual. It was marvellous. I won't say that the tree spoke to me. It was quite a young tree, after all, and me being new and everything. But I can imagine it might if I were away from people with shopping trolleys.

Hugging trees has a calming effect on me. I'm talking about enormous trees that will be there when we are all dead and gone. I've hugged trees in every part of this little island.

Gerry Adams

July 7

Time

The amazing thing is that every atom in your body came from a star that exploded.

Lawrence M. Krauss

I used to be a rock. A piece of granite-like rock, I rather think. I was happy. I thought I would last forever. And now, here I am in this relatively (by comparison) frail body and I am happy here. I know this body will not last forever.

That does not concern me. I shall continue on my journey. Forever changing, forever being.

It is so good to be.

I do enjoy it.

Thank you for sharing this instant with me.

We should learn to savour some moments to let time feel worth existing.

Munia Khan

Thinking

To think too much is a disease.

Fyodor Dostoyevsky

Sometimes, often at night, but during the day too, my ego likes to drop bomb thoughts into my head. They can consume me as I look at them from every possible and impossible angle.

There are two ways I have found to disarm or remove them. One is to say, "I'm not going to think about that anymore," and then get on with something else.

A second way is that when I'm thinking about anything, its image is in front of me so that I can see it. So I pick the idea up and put it behind my head. Then, as I can't see it, it no longer bothers me.

If the "worry" is something I need to address, I say, "I won't think about this again until 9 a.m. or whenever". Then when 9 a.m. comes, I will find the rational solutions and actions I have been looking for. Occasionally I may have to get rid of the thought two or three times, but never more than three before it is gone.

Don't get too deep, it leads to over-thinking, and overthinking leads to problems that don't even exist in the first place.

Jayson Engay

Employment

If you don't make things happen, things will happen to you.

Robert Collier

You are self-employed. Most people think that they have jobs and that there is some kind of security with their job.

If you ask people who have a job if they are self-employed, most will say 'no'.

It is a mistake to assume that we have a job. That we have any right to job security.

We are all employed by ourselves. We answer to ourselves. So we want to be enthusiastic about whatever we do. And do it wholeheartedly as if its success depends upon us because it does.

Our success, the joy we may achieve, totally depends on us. We want to go to bed tonight feeling good about ourselves and looking forward to tomorrow.

And, of course, this is reflected in every area of our life.

Luck is what happens when preparation meets opportunity.

Seneca

Expectations

Expectations were like fine pottery. The harder you held them, the more likely they were to crack.

Brandon Sanderson

The mother of a friend of mine was a net curtain twitcher. She was constantly peering and peaking at the world. Sucking her teeth as she expected the worst to happen.

And it did, of course, to her and her family.

Why do people expect the worst? Why do people fear sending their children or themselves out into the world to have adventures? If you think about it, all successes have come about because someone took a risk.

Imagine, for a moment, setting sail from Spain across the ocean leading to the earth's edge.

Go out, take risks. Live.

Maybe sometimes it's riskier not to take a risk. Sometimes all you're guaranteeing is that things will stay the same.

Danny Wallace

Moving On

The biggest problem any of us ever face is our own negative thinking.

Robert Schuller

Somewhere along the way, I stopped processing negatives. I do not carry bad things forward with me. I forget that I was ill. I don't notice lousy weather. If something bad or less good happens to me, I move on from it. I do not allow it to fester inside me and poison my being.

How did I do this? That is a difficult question because it happens so automatically now. The weather is easy to do. I'm happy to be in it, experiencing it, whatever it is. I choose to be grateful that I'm alive and can be rained on.

There were years when I didn't do any of this, and I lived in a world of blackness and pain.

I have learnt to let go of the negatives that life or people throw at me. I step sideways and disengage from them and get on with living my life in peace and happiness.

My motto is never hold onto anything. I accept and then let go: not just the negatives, but the praise too, or it'll get to my head.

Nargis Fakhri

Thinking

Misery is almost always the result of thinking.

Joseph Joubert

We are addicted to our thoughts. We cannot change anything if we cannot change our thinking.

Santosh Kalwar

Most of the time, we think with our heads – the place where our ego lives and barks out its awfulness at us.

I agree, not all the time. We can and probably do bumble quite happily along, blissfully unaware of the next blow it will deliver. But when it does deliver it, it does so with an elegant force that can create indescribable suffering.

If you go into your chest, your heart, you will find that you can think from there. (Yes, you can.)

And if you do that now, you will realise that everything feels different.

And you can continue to think, talk, and act with your heart for as long as you want. Oh, and have you noticed that the ego isn't there? Good, eh?

Of course, it's waiting in your head for you to return because you will, as it is your habit.

But the more time you spend thinking, talking, and being with your heart, the more of a habit that will become.

Did you ever stop to think, and forget to start again?

Winnie the Pooh. A. A. Milne

July 13

Clothes

Be uniquely you. Stand out. Be colourful. The world needs your prismatic soul!

Amy Leigh Mercree

Do yourself a favour
Throw away all your black and navy-blue clothes.
Yes, I did say that.
Okay, do it over the next three months.
It brings you down when you get up in the morning and put on black, navy or dark grey clothes.
When you put on colours and look in the mirror, it lifts your soul, your being.
If you don't believe me do it a handful of times, and you will notice the difference in your day and your well-being.
Go on! Be brave! Live!
Enjoy.
P.S. If you come to my funeral, wear the brightest clothes you can.

Colours make nature pulsate with life.

Michael Bassey Johnson

Waiting

I have noticed that the people who are late are often so much jollier than the people who have to wait for them.

E. V. Lucas

What do you do while you are waiting for people? When I was young and arranged to meet friends on some corner or outside a place, I always got there on time or early.

One day I decided I would never wait for anyone longer than 15 minutes, and I've stuck to that pretty well. I must mention that this was before mobile phones.

Now, when I am waiting, I relax and go into the moment and enjoy it rather than getting agitated. I do some kind of happy meditation. Or if I'm at home, I just get on with my life.

I refuse to let other people dominate the way I feel. Only I can do that. And I choose to feel good, most of the time, I prefer that. My aim in life is to enjoy myself.

If you wait for perfect conditions, you will never get anything done.

Ecclesiastes

Compassion

Love and compassion are necessities, not luxuries. Without them, humanity cannot survive.

Dalai Lama

One of our problems is that we are not compassionate with ourselves. We frequently find little niggles that increase our feelings of less than.

And even if you cannot identify a single one now, you know that you have had feelings of failure.

(My ego is shouting out at me, but they are all perfect, it is only you who has doubts and lacks self-belief. "You cannot write this. They are confident within themselves, and their lives are perfect. Stop. Stop. Write something else. Do not put this in the book. They will read it and throw the book away").

And all I am suggesting is that we gently, gracefully, quietly take a handful of seconds now to forgive ourselves our imperfections. We accept other people's imperfections without giving them a thought (most of the time). Let's go easy on ourselves too. Do something for me, hug yourself and say, "I love you."

There, I've written it.

One love, one heart, one destiny.

Bob Marley

Reflections

The outside world reflects our inner world. Always. And forever.

Karen Casey

A friend told me the other day that she didn't know when her ego was controlling her thinking or when her inner being (god) was in control.

It struck me as interesting that she realised that something was in control, something other than herself. Few people ever come to that depth of understanding.

The truth is, of course, that whenever we are judgemental, critical or negative in any way, our ego has us in its grasp.

And every judgemental thought we have is a reflection of ourselves. We are creating a world where negativity rules.

Whereas when we are being loving, forgiving or accepting, god or our inner being is guiding us.

Life is a mirror, and you see in it the reflection of your inner self.

Waqi Munim

We do not learn from experience. We learn from reflecting on experience.

John Dewey

Sexism

Most men fear getting laughed at or humiliated by a romantic prospect, while most women fear rape and death.

Gavin de Becker

Oh god, you're not going to write this are you? Are you sure...

The vast majority of men say sexist things, disrespecting women. You might almost say that their mindset has been bred into them.

Maybe you don't do this. If not, bravo. But come with me for a moment into your home or your street. You are with your young daughter, aged, let's say, 10-14. Think about the words that men say, the words they call women, the way they brag, the way they label women as sexual objects, that's good and bad sexual objects, and think, do you want your beautiful daughter to hear that?

Is that the world you want her to be growing up in and experiencing? And so, even if you never say anything crass, vulgar, degrading, shaming, or disgusting yourself, if you listen to others saying anything of that sort, you are party to the words and the attitude.

Every time it happens, it strengthens the belief that this is okay.

So whenever we hear it, we want to challenge or somehow stop it. That is the only way we will achieve liberation.

The emotional, sexual, and psychological stereotyping of females begins when the doctor says: "It's a girl".

Shirley Chisholm

Advice

*Advice is like snow, the softer it falls, the longer it dwells
upon, and the deeper it sinks into the mind.*

Samuel Taylor Coleridge

Many receive advice, only the wise profit from it.

Harper Lee

Sometimes, when people come to us with their problems and challenges, we edit what we honestly think to avoid offending them.

We find comfortable words. We say, "I think you should do this," but we say it in such a way as to let them believe that there is a choice in the matter. And that's okay if we are unsure of ourselves.

There are times, though, when we know at some truly deep level what the answer is, and when that happens, we want to say what we think.

Say it forcibly, not worrying about how it will be received or what they think about us.

We want to open our mouth and let the words out. If we don't, they will continue to suffer because no one has had the guts to tell them the truth.

*I see it perfectly: there are two possible situations, one can
either do this or that. My honest opinion and my friendly
advice is this: do it or do not do it – you will regret both.*

Soren Kierkegaard

July 19

Focus

It is not for me to judge another man's life. I must judge, I must choose, I must spurn, purely for myself. For myself alone.

Hermann Hesse

It is so easy to shuffle through our days and lives only focusing on the less good.

As you walk down the street, noticing the potholes, the chewing gum, the inconsiderate drivers, and the face-masked people exuding fear.

Or in life, picking up on the shortcomings and failures of others and getting lost in their trouble, deceit, and selfishness.

Put a black dot on a piece of paper and ask people what they see? They almost always say the black dot and not the expanse of white paper.

And so it is with us. We focus on the things that are wrong, the bad people, the disasters to such an extent that we cease to see beauty, stop dancing through our lives but shuffle instead.

But yes, as you know, we have a choice. Which choice shall we make today?

Very occasionally, if you pay really close attention, life doesn't suck.

Joss Whedon

July 20

Acceptance

*An open-minded person sees life without boundaries,
whereas a close-minded person can only see what's beyond
their eyes.*

Mark Twain

An open mind is like an open window, it lets the fresh air in.

Mike Hernacki

Most of us probably think that we are open-minded. That
we, by and large, tolerate other people's opinions and beliefs.
However, if we are honest, most of us have things, people,
and attitudes that we find totally unacceptable at best and
challenging at worst.

But, if we want to enjoy freedom and peace of mind, we
want to find a way to accept others however they are.

We find this difficult because we spend our lives judging
ourselves and failing. And so we take the judgement out into
the world and find fault there.

If we learn to accept our imperfections and forgive
ourselves, we will slowly discover that we can take our
acceptance out into the world.

*Until the mind is open, the heart stays closed. The open
mind is the key to the open heart.*

Byron Katie

*The mind that opens to a new idea never comes back to its
original size.*

Albert Einstein

July 21

Love

They did normal things, but they did them with abnormal love and inclusiveness.

Donna Goddard

There is something extraordinary about the love a child and a grandparent share. It has purity. (Okay, not always, but you know what I mean.) It is not cluttered with all the baggage that so often accompanies love.

So often, love is confused by sex and looks.

It comes along with desires and expectations. And that can be wonderful, but it will only continue to be wonderful if we accept that love is much more than that.

You look at elderly overweight couples and cannot imagine that they can be in love. They surely must just exist together out of habit or fear.

But the thing that we don't realise is that true love is spiritual.

Yes, his or her habits are unbelievably frustrating, but if we have true spiritual love, then their shortcomings do not matter.

So, how many attributes of the person you love can you peel away and still love them? It is worth considering.

Worth discovering because if you are genuinely in love, that transcends everything. And if you are not in love, then perhaps it is time to move on before the door slams forever.

Whatever we are devoted to, we merge with.

Donna Goddard

July 22

Meditation

Nature does not hurry, yet everything is accomplished.

Lao Tzu

There are times when we find it easier to meditate than others. Times when it is a struggle to switch off all the commotion we are swimming in.

Sometimes, we sit, but we cannot honestly call that meditation. Our inner turmoil never abates.

Sometimes we really concentrate on meditating, but the real benefits still elude us.

In all those times when our meditation is less than, the cause is that we are trying at some level to do it.

Or we may even just be sitting, with the words of the meditation vibrating on our eardrums, but we cannot process them.

Rather than struggling with it, if we decide to allow ourselves to go in at the start of the meditation and just allow it to happen. We shall find that we get more benefit from it.

Your goal is not to battle with the mind, but to witness the mind.

Swami Muktananda

Time

How did it get so late so soon?

Dr Seuss

A man who dares to waste one hour of time has not discovered the value of life.

Charles Darwin

How many days have you got left on the earth?

Wow, that is a question, isn't it?

It makes us realise that we do not know. All these things we haven't been bothered to do, all these people we haven't given our love to, all the time we have wasted doing the dull recurring drudge, all those dreams we have never taken a step towards.

How many days have you got left?

What if it were only one?

You don't know if it's only one, of course, but suppose you were to have the slightest nudge or hint that it might be.

What will you fit into today to make it memorable? Whom will you call? What will you say? How will you change your behaviour toward your loved ones?

That is probably overload, so pick one thing to do differently today to make a difference.

(If you decide to call your Mum, don't burst into tears when you're talking to her. It is odds on that you will still be around tomorrow.)

Don't spend time beating on a wall, hoping to transform it into a door.

Coco Chanel

Time flies like an arrow, fruit flies like a banana.

Anthony G. Oettinger

Disagreements

An eye for an eye will only make the whole world blind.

Mahatma Gandhi

I think it's odd that grown-ups quarrel so easily and so often about such petty matters. Up to now, I always thought bickering was just something children did, and that they outgrew it.

Anne Frank

Sometimes, being human, we choose to get into arguments.

It all happens so quickly that we may feel that it was not a choice but a choice it was.

And on we charge, deeper and deeper, both or all of us digging frantically as we get into it.

And, of course, our ego loves this. "Bring it on", it cries, even when we are losing.

And I know, from personal experience (weepy face), that this is true.

I also know I can stop it as easily as clapping my hands.

I disengage and choose peace. Peace is inside me. Still. Quiet. Always there.

And when I choose peace, everything changes, not only for me but for other people. I am no longer a barrier that they can attack. And you cannot hit something that is not there.

And was it something worth fighting over anyway? Nearly always not.

There is peace.

Whenever you are confronted with an opponent. Conquer him with love.

Mahatma Gandhi

Guiding

You cannot change another person's mind or educate them, this they must do themselves.

Bryant McGill

So often, we want other people to do things. We want our children to achieve and maybe become... We want colleagues to change the way they... We want our friends or partner to...

And none of that is necessarily bad. Except they are on their own road. If we guide, push, or influence others, we may restrict their growth and incorrectly influence their path.

I know, I know, of course, your intentions are good. I know, I know, that you are only helping them in the right direction. I know, I know, that you only have their best interests at heart.

However, there is often just a teeny-weeny bit of self-interest there. Even if it is only "My daughter is a doctor".

And it is self-interest that is the danger.

It is so important that people have freedom, follow their path, and learn by making their own mistakes.

And it is also important that we allow ourselves freedom too.

Go! Have the adventure. The world will not end.

When dealing with people, let us remember that we are not dealing with creatures of logic. We are dealing with creatures of emotion.

Dale Carnegie

July 26

Reacting

Life is 10% what happens to you and 90% how you react to it.

Charles R. Swindoll

We do negative emotions with our body, intensifying the feeling and the insanity that accompanies it.

We tend to process many of our positive feelings verbally, acknowledging them fleetingly and moving on. "Lovely to see you", "That tastes good", "Look how beautiful..." and then on with our day.

If we swap these responses around and process the negatives fleetingly and the positives with our body, the change is extraordinary.

He cut me up, becomes. He must be in a hurry.

She didn't reply. She must be busy.

Whatever happens, if we don't let the negative into our body, it will damage us far less.

And when we see or talk to someone we love, if we fill our bodies with the feeling of love, we will flourish.

If we taste the food and intensify how wonderful the feeling of the taste is, or if we look at the flower and the sky and fill our body with the total delight and wonder of the experience, then we will be living.

Living rather than existing.

The possibilities are numerous once we decide to act and not react.

George Bernard Shaw

Love

Some of us learned early on that there is no facelift that works better than love, that nothing clears the sinuses better than a kiss, and there is no pension plan to compare with the prospect of spending your years with someone who promises to love honour and cherish you.

Lois Wyse

I love you.

I love you as you read my book

I love your existence.

Not in the way that I love my wife, sister, or son, but I love you.

So easy to walk down the road judging people.

So much more wonderful to walk down the road filled with love and bathe all the people we pass with love.

Not easy to do at first. After all, it requires effort, but it does become easier. We judge people without effort. It is second nature to us, and we are good at it.

The world changes when we love it.

It is a better place to live in.

Give until it hurts, because real love hurts.

Mother Teresa

Advice

Don't ever take a fence down until you know why it was up.

G. K. Chesterton

Hey, do you want something for free?

Or maybe just cheap?

You can get it at any old street corner if you hang around long enough.

Oh, and you can give it away too. Your generosity knows no bounds.

It's advice.

It is so easy to sort out other people's troubles like a hot knife slicing through butter.

And I am not saying that giving or receiving advice is wrong, just that much of it is useless.

The trouble with our problems is that we are emotionally attached to them, so we cannot see them. The next problem is that many of us ask endless people for advice until we find someone who tells us what we want to hear, and then we go and do 'that'.

I believe that we want to find one person whom we trust completely and discuss our lives with them. We may choose not to take their advice on all matters, which is okay because we know what we need to do more often than not. We just don't want to do it.

We grow by taking risks, not by hiding away.

Nobody can give you wiser advice than yourself.

Marcus Tullius Cicero

Never miss a good chance to shut up.

Will Rogers

Perspective

One person's craziness is another person's reality.

Tim Burton

The only thing you sometimes have control over is perspective. You don't have control over your situation. But you have a choice about how you view it.

Chris Pine

Sometimes we struggle. We don't enjoy what we are doing. Or how we feel. We crave some fix or object or attention or love or... add your own.

If, perchance, there is anything in your life that is not perfect at the moment. Please bring it to mind, into your being and feel the disquiet/pain it is causing you now.

Okay, look up into the corner of the room you are in. Go up there and look down at yourself, wherever you are. Look at yourself and the things around you from up there. And tell me, what has happened to the negative feelings you had?

They have gone. When we are not in our body, we do not feel the emotions in our body.

So if we have a job we don't like, we can do it perfectly well without being in our body and experiencing our dislike. If we crave something to change the way we feel, then if we are out of our body, looking at ourselves, the feeling is not there.

The challenge, of course, is staying out, because our ego wants us back in there, suffering, craving, and indulging. But knowing that, we can let go of the unwanted desire, float up and look calmly down.

(Oh, and we want to be talking to other people about our challenges, or we don't stand a chance.)

The greatest tragedy for any human being is going through their entire lives believing the only perspective that matters is their own.

Doug Baldwin

Patience

Patience and perseverance have a magical effect before which difficulties disappear, and obstacles vanish.

John Quincy Adams

Patience is a virtue
So we are told.

And it is true that when things are not going where or as quickly as we would like, impatience flutters or blasts its way into our body. It may be in our mind, but it is in our body that we are damaging ourselves.

If we can learn to let things take their course and not get stressed about them, everything is so much better.

And the thing we are impatient about will either happen, or it won't, and it will be irrelevant anyway in a day or two.

If you want to make a call to find out what is going on, do so, but do it with ease and grace. It really doesn't matter.

A man who is master of patience is master of everything else.

George Savile

Struggle

You need to spend time crawling alone through shadows to truly appreciate what it is to stand in the sun.

Shaun Hick

When we are having a hard time and struggling, our natural tendency is to withdraw.

Admittedly some people spread all their shit liberally around to anyone who will listen. But more often than not, they are just slinging all their troubles about, not believing that anyone can help them. Whether they realise it or not, their real desire is to bring everyone down to their level.

So when we are struggling, we slam the doors, isolate, withdraw into the "poor me's", and quietly increase our suffering.

The solution is simple. Take your eyes off yourself and go and help others. Your problems begin to crumble away.

Of course, the difficulty is that we don't want to do it. A core part of us wants to be depressed or unhappy, and until the pain becomes intense enough, we may be unable to motivate ourselves to do anything about it.

Although being reminded of this may enable us to get out of it sooner.

Never throughout history has a man who lived a life of ease left a name worth remembering.

Theodore Roosevelt

Life's a climb, but the view is great.

Miley Cyrus

Don't
Complain

Don't
Explain

Emotions

She was a stranger in her own life, a tourist in her own body.

Melissa de la Cruz

We say things like I am sad, I am depressed, I am happy, I am overwhelmed. They are not true – none of them. Go outside of yourself and see yourself in the room you are in. Look at yourself. There you are. What you are looking at is not depression or happiness (whatever they may be). What you are looking at is you.

We clasp the emotions and pull them over us like cloaks, but they are not who we are. We are not the clothes we wear, the car we drive, or the house we live in.

We are vibrant living beings. Magnificent.

The emotions, good or bad, come and go. Realising that we do not become them makes it much easier to get on without the feelings we don't want and enjoy the good more fully.

The attempt to escape from pain, is what creates more pain.

Gabor Maté

August 2

Breathing

I don't mind if you want to start ranting just as long as you understand I'll be ignoring every word.

Suzanne Wright

Not my circus, not my monkeys

Polish Proverb

A calm, still mind is lovely.

And yet so much of the time, it can be closer to the roar of ranting and madness.

Maybe nothing as bad as that for you, but is it as calm as you would like it to be?

Our trouble these days is that we are programmed to charge on. We choose the quick fix, a tablet, or no fix, just throw another twig on the blaze.

Interestingly, it changes or even stops our thinking when we hold our breath.

So deep breath in. In. In.

Hold it, hold it.

Let it all out.

Hold the emptiness.

Hold it, hold it, hold it.

Repeat as many times as you want to feel good.

One of the nice things about this is that you can do it as an exercise and stop doing everything. Or you can do it quietly without any fuss, without drawing attention to yourself, while you are with other people.

The only difficulty, the challenge about the whole thing, is remembering to do it. Oh, and then doing it. So much easier to take a tablet or blunder deeper into discomfort.

There is a calmness to a life lived in gratitude, a quiet joy.

Ralph H. Blum

Stop

Stop. Revive. Survive.

Melina Marchetta

Be in this moment now, wholly.
Just be.
Stop.
Accept yourself in this moment.
Be at peace.
Take a breath.
Be aware of yourself.
No past.
No future.
Here now.

There, if you are doing this now, you are untroubled. You have oneness with yourself. You can do it, you can repeat it.

All our turmoil, that is, ALL our turmoil, comes from the past or the future. There is no turmoil now. There is peace.

Breathe.

If you want a happy ending, that depends, of course, on where you stop your story.

Orson Welles

Change

Everything changes and, somewhere along the line, I'm changing with it.

Eric Burdon

The only constant thing in the universe is change. Everything comes and goes. We are fleeting seconds of time.

Which is a little scary. Except it does not feel like that to us. It can drag on interminably.

When things are going right, and we want them to go on forever, they don't. When things are going badly, it can feel as if it will last forever.

However, both the good and the bad will pass, which should fill us with joy.

We learn as we go. We look back at our good times and our struggles with gratitude. Now we have new wisdom to share with ourselves and with others.

If you have struggles, take the time to relax into them, however bad the situation. Allow yourself to feel gratitude for it. Thank it (however hard this is). Your perception will change, and you will find it easier to move through it.

Nothing lasts forever. And that includes the future. That doesn't last forever either.

Today was good.
Today was fun.
Tomorrow is.
Another one.

Dr Seuss

Struggle

Where there is no struggle, there is no strength.

Oprah Winfrey

I know that you have times of self-doubt and blackness.
Times when the struggle seems overwhelming.

I know this because this is how we all travel through our lives. And we look at others and have no idea of the extent of their difficulties. If only we could realise that others are struggling massively too.

Remember, what we crave is love. Go inside yourself and embrace yourself with love.

Allow the love to flow into every part of our being completely.

What then?

Struggle teaches you a lot of things, and I am happy that I witnessed a roller coaster ride. The journey has improved me as a person and made me more mature.

Manoj Bajpayee

A dog is the only thing on earth that loves you more than he loves himself.

Josh Billings

Experience

Nothing is a waste of time if you use the experience wisely.

Auguste Rodin

In this instant, this is the first time you are doing, experiencing, and living this. Whatever it is. Always.

Even if you are doing something for the millionth time, each time is unique. It only happens once. It is special.

And so, if we were clever, we would surely want to be present and experience the happening we are in.

How many mouthfuls of coffee, tea, soda, beer, water, etc., do you take a day? Maybe you enjoy savouring one. Perhaps none?

And yet, if you pick up the cup. Feel your lips on it, feel the liquid as it goes into your mouth and onto your tongue. And enjoy?

Or as you walk down the road and you look, smell, feel, touch, listen, are present in the experience, what incredible richness.

Every moment is an experience.

Jake Roberts

Inner Being

Enjoy the peace of nature and declutter your inner world.

Amit Ray

Today I'd like to offer you a space in your life. A chance to reconnect with yourself. Your true self.

There is a "you", an inner you, that you were born with. And throughout your life, you and the people you have met have done their best to cage it.

But it is there inside of you.

A light burning.

It has made its presence felt to you during your life. It has given you a few seconds, minutes or even an hour or two of being unfettered.

Able to act, and say, and be the honest you.

Then you have snapped the door shut on it and returned to conformity.

Do not fear it. Do not suppress it. Revel in it. Give yourself freedom and joy.

I do not need to tell you how to do this, you know. However, you think you do not. The way is through stillness and allowing yourself to be. Let the thoughts, the words, and the actions out.

Live.

Desperation is the raw material of drastic change. Only those who can leave behind everything they have ever believed in can hope to escape.

William S. Burroughs

A good traveller is one who knows how to travel with the mind.

Michael Bassey Johnson

Self-belief

I will never be an old man. To me, old age is always 15 years older than I am.

Francis Bacon

Our unconscious mind does not grow old. Our bodies age, and because of tradition or expectation, we tend to buy into the idea that we are older and expect to find things "difficult" and that we ought to be "slowing down".

But our unconscious doesn't age. Of course, it will oblige if we treat it like a doddery old fool.

But if we continue to expect it to function magnificently, it will do so eagerly. It can go on being as sharp as ever.

So never treat yourself or anyone else as if they are getting old. It is locking them in a cage and throwing away the key. And you do not want that existence, do you?

Your parents showed you the world, and in return, you showed them the old age home.

Anonymous.

Acting

To grasp the full significance of life is the actor's duty, to interpret it is his problem, and to express it is his dedication.

Marlon Brando

We have our roles in this world, our lives. Our roles are who we are and what we have to do in life.

It is easier to make our way through our challenges when we accept this is true. Any difficulties we face are just part of the role we have chosen.

We will live through them.

Instead of fighting against life and being overwhelmed with fear or anger, we want to remember that we are the actors in a play. When this scene is over, we will move to the next and the one beyond that.

Our job is to play our part in the present scene as best we can.

I think you should take your job seriously, but not yourself.' That is the best combination.

Dame Judi Dench

If you always put limits on everything you do, physical or anything else, it will spread into your work and into your life. There are no limits. There are only plateaus, and you must not stay there, you must go beyond them.

Bruce Lee

Indifference

The worst sin towards our fellow creatures is not to hate them, but to be indifferent to them, that's the essence of inhumanity.

George Bernard Shaw

Emotion. Full-blown raw emotion, good or bad, awakens us.

Destructive, negative, hostile anger or hatred consumes us like petrol burning uncontrollably and fills us with poison. It is something we know we don't want and can avoid with the help of meditation and inner peace.

While genuine unconditional love fills us with joy and contentment.

It is easy to disregard people whom we do not greatly care about. We listen to their problems without listening, offer advice without thinking, or wander away without connecting.

And yet, you are with them for a reason. A reason greater than you.

We are all interconnected, so when we are with people, we want to give them our full attention.

We will be rewarded. Maybe not by them, but in some way. And in fact, it does not matter whether we are rewarded or not. We owe them, and the world, the gift of ourselves.

To go to bed at night knowing that today you have done all you could have done is a gift beyond words.

Desire is half of life, indifference is half of death.

Kahlil Gibran

Perception

It's not what you look at that matters, it's what you see.

Henry David Thoreau

How I perceive the world and myself is my way of doing it. Nobody else does it in the same way.

My perception of the world and myself is not set in stone. I can choose to change it. I can become open to the idea of change. I can begin to look for clues about how other people view things.

I can even take a belief that I have, that I've always had perhaps, and peel back the layers that keep it locked in and then question it. I can if I choose, change it. And if we change one perception, it is easier to change another.

My perceptions only exist in my mind. I can change them and always change them back if I prefer the old perception. So go into the world with an open mind.

Explore!

Enjoy.

Every man takes the limits of his own field of vision for the limits of the world.

Arthur Schopenhauer

The eyes see only what the mind is prepared to comprehend.

Robertson Davies

Soul

Let your soul stand cool and composed before a million universes.

Walt Whitman

The spirit never dies.

We are spirits in a temporary human container. Everything physical is in a state of transition. Ashes to ashes, dust to dust. Our bodies will change back into stardust. We used to be stardust, and we will be again. At least, this is true of our bodies. Our spirit is not stardust, and it moves on.

And so, to mourn the dead makes no sense.

Of course, we mourn that they are no longer with us. And yes, we miss them because we loved being with them. But what we are grieving is our loss, not theirs, because they are not lost.

How would they want us to be now? Happy or miserable? If you and they loved each other, they would like you to be happy.

So stop missing them. And stop torturing yourself with pain and grief.

Instead, when you think of them, think of them with joy. Do the things with them that you loved to do. Listen to music, look at the sky, the flowers, eat the food. Laugh at the jokes, and be overwhelmed with joy and happiness as you share what you did with them. Be happy, embrace and love life.

The cosmos is within us. We are made of star-stuff.

Carl Sagan

Liberation

*If you love someone, set them free. If they come back,
they're yours: If they don't, they never were.*

Richard Bach

I came downstairs this morning to find the most beautiful moth on my curtain. I carefully opened a window, and with even more care, I captured the moth in the palms of my hands. I took it to the open window and spread my hands. It stood there in all its magnificence. I imagined it looking up at me quietly, saying, "Thank you."

Then with a nod of its head, it flew out into the world. Into freedom without a backward glance.

After it had travelled three, maybe four meters from my window, a swallow flew by, gobbled up my moth, and flew off.

Is this all I have become? A swallow feeder?

I don't feed the birds because they need me; I feed the birds because I need them.

Kathi Hutton

Love

*Love looks not with the eyes but with the mind, and
therefore is winged Cupid painted blind.*

William Shakespeare – Midsummer Night's Dream

When we are in love, it is impossible to imagine that anyone has ever felt the way we do. What we have is so unique and utterly magical.

When we are not in love, we may have vague memories of what it was like, but when we look at other people who appear to be in love, we do not understand.

And, of course, there is all the confusion about sex. Being in love and sex are not the same thing. The passion of sex can be magnificent, and there is no denying that. But real unconditional love is a spiritual connection that transcends the physical. It is one spirit or soul sharing the embrace of another spirit or soul and has no demands. It is the total giving of oneself.

Love her but leave her wild.

Atticus

*Nothing you become will disappoint me; I have no
preconception that I'd like to see you be or do. I have no
desire to force you, only to discover you. You can't
disappoint me.*

Mary Haskell

Love

Let no one who loves be called altogether unhappy. Even love unreturned has its rainbow.

J. M. Barrie

We all want to be loved. And we seek confirmation that the important people in our lives love us.

And sometimes, when they don't do what we want, our ego jumps in and says, "See, he/she doesn't love you anymore".

And then we dive into the mess of questioning things and looking for proof. Meddling.

If, instead, we focus on offering love, everything will be better.

Giving is the only way to receive more.

Lailah Gifty Akita

August 16

Death

Charlie: Someday, we will all die, Snoopy.

Snoopy: True, but on all the other days, we will not.

Charles M. Schulz

Spoiler Alert! We are all going to die. The richest, the happiest, the poorest, the most miserable people you know will all die.

We are all the same that way.

And we are all the same in so many more ways than we realise or can imagine.

We judge ourselves against others, even if only unconsciously, and think we are better or worse than they are.

But none of it really matters. It only matters to our ego, who uses the judgements to make us different.

We are not different.

Accepting this at a core level changes how we view and experience the world. It makes our journey through it so much easier. We are all going to die.

The truth I have been seeking – this truth is Death. Yet Death is also a seeker. Forever seeking me. So – we meet at last. And I am prepared. I am at peace.

Bruce Lee

Time

When was the last time you spent a quiet moment just doing nothing – just sitting and looking at the sea, or watching the wind blowing the tree limbs, or waves rippling on a pond, a flickering candle, or children playing in the park.

Ralph Marston

So how do you spend your time?

Productively? Creatively? Usefully? Imaginatively?

Apparently not, if you are average.

On average, we spend three to four months a year watching TV and on our phones.

Yes, that's three to four months!

Worth considering.

Just take a little bit of that time to do something that requires creativity and stimulation. What then might you achieve?

It's your life.

Use it as you will.

If you spend too much time thinking about a thing, you'll never get it done.

Bruce Lee

August 18

Love

There is no fear when you choose love. The more you choose love, the more love is in your life. It gets easier and easier.

Melissa Etheridge

Think for a moment of someone you (let's say) struggle with, one of the most difficult people in your life.

And now, allow yourself a trace of a smile as you feel love within. Let it spread throughout your body, and when it is there, think about them again.

The way you view them will have changed. It is better.

"Light bulb moment."

If you can do that now, you can do it as you go through your day.

And guess what? Your day will be so much better.

Spread love everywhere you go. Let no one ever come to you without leaving happier.

Mother Teresa

Rituals

There is comfort in rituals, and rituals provide a framework for stability, when you are trying to find answers.

Deborah Norville

Ritual is important. All religions have rituals to bring them closer to their God.

And we, yes, humble old us, whether we believe or not, we are strengthened by rituals. By sitting down with our God and accessing the peace that goes with that. If we do not currently have a practice that includes quiet reflection, we are cheating ourselves out of potential peace.

And if we do have rituals or prayers, are we accessing them fully or just doing them by rote, without thought or connection? If so, they are pretty useless, and we might want to consider being more involved with them. The mindless beating of a drum does not create music.

Rituals are magical.

André Aciman

Presence

*The most precious gift we can offer others is our attention.
When mindfulness embraces those we love, they will bloom
like flowers.*

Thich Nhat Hanh

I sometimes think our minds are like confetti blown in the wind.

So many bits, all hurrying, all crying out for attention, all so important to themselves.

And when we are with someone, it is so easy to let them and what they are saying become another confetti, whizzing around amongst the others after just a few moments.

But if we decide to give them our full attention when we are with them, the confetti disappears. We become centred. We are present. They benefit. And we benefit too. So much. So very much.

Our attention may only last a little while, but we can come back again. And the more often we do this, the less effort it is and the longer it lasts. Until it ceases to be an effort, it becomes what we do. We will have more peace in our life.

*Appreciation is the highest form of prayer, for it
acknowledges the presence of good wherever you shine the
light of your thankful thoughts.*

Alan Cohen

Your children need your presence more than your presents.

Jesse Jackson

Courage

I've got the wisdom. It's the courage I lack.

Bob God

We know what we need to do. At some deep level, we know the truth. We don't need advice. We just need courage. We may think we need guidance, perhaps so that we can do it elegantly. But getting advice is just a delaying tactic so that we never have to face up to doing things.

Bummer.

Now you know. But there are still things you don't want to do.

Of course you don't. "And does it really matter anyway?" You cry.

Well, yes, it does. We want to live comfortably with ourselves.

However, most people go to the grave without having the courage to do the things that need doing. Were they happy?

So don't we owe it to ourselves to have courage?

Only those who will risk going too far can possibly find out how far one can go.

T. S. Eliot

Focus

It is during our darkest moments that we must focus to see the light.

Aristotle Onassis

I have a puppy called... you will not be surprised to hear... Joy.

I am currently house-training her to do her business outside. A delightful job...

I'm out with her, and whilst she does her poo, she is constantly sniffing the ground and moving forwards to find a more exciting smell.

"Concentrate on one end at a time", I call out to her. (I don't think she understands.)

It occurred to me that this is what we so easily do, think about other things rather than concentrating on what we are doing. We do not give ourselves to the job at hand, so it, and we, suffer.

What you stay focused on will grow.

Roy T. Bennett

Energy

Sometimes we lack energy. Everything seems just too much effort. We shuffle along, doing the bare necessities to move our life into the next day, but with no joy. With no appetite.

We often arrive at feeling like this because of some illness or depression or simply because the joy and light have left our lives.

You may not even remember a time like this. But most of us suffer from it to a greater or lesser extent.

If the idea of changing this attracts us (even a little), the best thing to do is to think of one thing that needs doing. Don't go into the doing. Rather travel ahead and see the task completed. Everything finished and looking wonderful. And then, keeping that image in mind, arise, start and do it. Do it with pleasure.

Keep your face always towards the sunshine – and the shadows will fall behind you.

Walt Whitman

Freedom

You won't find freedom in the world because it does not exist in the world.

Geoff Thompson

Does that bother you? Is freedom something you search for or even think about, or do you just travel relatively peacefully towards tomorrow?

And what about others? What do you think they are doing? Anything? Nothing? Are they searching?

And if freedom doesn't exist in the world? If it only exists within us? Do we choose to claim it? Ever? Often? Never?

So many questions.

What do you want?

Freedom?

Or no freedom?

Freedom is the foundation of all wonderful things in life.

Jeffrey Tucker

No one is free, even the birds are chained to the sky.

Bob Dylan

August 25

Thoughts

Risk comes from not knowing what you're doing.

Warren Buffett

I wonder if you've ever seen a murmuration of starlings? When thousands fly as one, in the same way that fishes do, when predators are attacking them.

(If you haven't seen a murmuration, it is worth looking at one online.)

I was fortunate enough to watch one the other day at dusk and saw a pair of crows flying, I imagined, just getting on with the business of going home. I presumed that the starlings didn't even notice the crows, while the crows could not fail to notice the starlings. And if that was the case, what would they be saying?

That they thought the starlings were just stupid show-offs? They looked down on anyone who just mindlessly followed the masses? The starlings clearly couldn't have any sense to behave like that, it could only lead to doom?

So are you a crow or a starling?

What do you think?

And is that the right thing to be thinking?

I write because I don't know what I think until I read what I say.

Flannery O'Connor

Selfishness

Selfishness is not living as one wishes to live, it is asking others to live as one wishes to live.

Oscar Wilde

People don't want other people to be people.

Gene Wolfe

Selfishness and greed, individual or national, cause most of our troubles.

Harry S. Truman

Are you selfish?

Do you believe things should be done a certain way and get annoyed if they are not done like that?

When something around the house needs doing, do you do it, or do you wait for it to be done?

Do you think the things that matter to you are more important than the things that matter to others?

Do you think what can I do to make the lives of the people I'm with more pleasant? Do you nearly always choose what is watched on TV? Do you eat without helping to create it or clear it up? Do you laugh at sexist jokes? Any "Yes's" there?

You are selfish.

A man is called selfish not for pursuing his own good but for neglecting his neighbour's.

Richard Whately

Serenity

Do your work, then step back. The only path to serenity.

Lao Tzu

Ah yes, serenity... I remember... It was nice, good, wonderful even... but life... well... life...

Oh, the turmoil, the rushing, the coping, the idiots beeping their horns, the people pushing past, the mindless, the banal, the news, the binge-watch, the children, the parents, the world!

All so hard to struggle through. And for each one, there are another ten not mentioned. How can anyone cope? If only... yes, if only...

Ah yes, serenity...

If I can remember to breathe... Slowly... Slower... Even slower... Even slower than that... Just for a few seconds...

And go into that inner peace.

Ah yes... Serenity... So good...

Which do I prefer? Which is better? Which will I choose to spend more time with? You can't decide for me. Only I can choose for myself. You can't make me feel anything. Only I can do that.

You find peace not by rearranging the circumstances of your life, but by realising who you are at the deepest level.

Eckhart Tolle

Self-respect

When you are content to be simply yourself and don't compare or compete, everyone will respect you.

Lao Tzu

My father used to get up and put on a tracksuit, and then later in the mornings, he'd dress properly in trousers and a shirt. Even when he was not planning to do anything, he did that, not expecting to leave the house or meet anyone.

"Why do you do that?" I asked him once.

"It makes the day real. It gives me self-respect. I feel like a human being."

So now, I do that, even when my expectation is of nothing.

It makes me feel alive.

Respect your efforts, respect yourself. Self-respect leads to self-discipline. When you have both firmly under your belt, that's real power.

Clint Eastwood

God's Children

I do believe that we're all God's children.

Octavia Spencer

We are all God's children.

It doesn't matter who or what we believe God to be. It doesn't matter what rules we believe God has or has not. It does not matter how we worship or if we do not worship.

We are all God's children, or none of us are.

The moment we say or think, "They are not doing it properly," we move from love to judgement, and we are then surely not behaving as God would want us to.

So love.

Be love.

Have peace and love.

When the voice of love speaks to you, it comes with courage.

Banning Liebscher

Where love is God is.

Henry Drummond

Resentments

I started realising how the condition of our hearts affects the way we see. If your heart is full of bitterness, anger and resentment, you're going to look at the world as a very evil place.

Danny Gokey

My puppy has several toys, some squeaky, some chewy, and her favourite is an empty plastic milk bottle. She bounds from one to another and back again as if afraid of missing out.

And that is what so many of us do at times in our life. We bounce from one distraction to another. And we toss one resentment aside for a little squeaky snippet of dislike to a large, noisy mouthful of rage.

Strange.

You'd think that we would know.

You'd think that we would have learnt by now.

When we do that, "they" or "it" are owning us. We have discarded our brain, consciousness, serenity, and peace of mind and handed the power over to "them."

At any moment, we can stop. We can reclaim power over ourselves and get on with enjoying our life.

So simple!!

So Easy.

Our fatigue is often caused not by work, but by worry, frustration and resentment.

Dale Carnegie

Desires

We cannot solve our problems with the same thinking that created them.

Albert Einstein

Without ice cream, there would be chaos and darkness.

Don Kardong

Do you ever feel or think... "I want something to change the way I feel?" More often than not, we don't even go into that thought. We just start searching for something.

It can be anything from a cup of tea, some new expensive toy, or our drug of choice. Our drug of choice may not be a drug. It could be exercise, food, gambling, or anger. But whatever it is, we are in some way addicted to it.

In the long term, to change that, we want to admit it to ourselves and another human being. Look at our lives and how we can become happy.

But in the short term, if we take three long, slow, deep breaths, the craving will disappear. Even if only for a short time. And it is possible to become addicted to three long, slow, deep breaths, which is good. They cost nothing and are not fattening.

Perfect happiness is the absence of striving for happiness.

Chuang-Tse

The perfect moment is filled with joy and happiness. If you are attentive, you will see it.

Thich Nhat Hanh

Keep

letting

go

September 1

Learning

Live as if you were to die tomorrow. Learn as if you were to live forever.

Mahatma Gandhi

We cannot learn anything until we are ready.

That's anything and everything.

Whether it is a new word, cooking an apple pie, or discarding self-doubt or anger. We cannot learn it until we are ready.

We may grasp it and do it for a little while, but until we are genuinely open, willing, and accepting, we will soon revert to not knowing, and the old behaviours will return.

And it's no good "trying" to do it. Trying is doomed before its starts. To learn something, we want to be relaxed and open and allow ourselves to embrace it.

Meditating and visualising ourselves succeeding helps too. Millions have already done it, and you can too.

The doer alone learneth.

Frederick Nietzsche

Smooth seas do not make skilful sailors.

African Proverb

Privileges

The privilege of a lifetime is being who you are.

Joseph Campbell

We have so many privileges in our lives.

So many that we just take them for granted without a thought.

Occasionally, or even more often, it is good to stop and consider all the fantastic things we take for granted. And then to say thank you and feel the gratitude.

When you arise in the morning, think of what a precious privilege it is to be alive, to breathe, to think, to enjoy, to love.

Marcus Aurelius

Expecting the world to treat you fairly because you are good is like expecting the bull not to charge because you are a vegetarian.

Dennis Wholey

Advice

Good advice is something a man gives when he is too old to set a bad example.

Francois de la Rochefoucauld

Ah yes, advice. Here it comes. Let's switch off our brains. More inflated wisdom is being dumped on us.

Of course, that isn't always the case, and sometimes advice does allow us to think aloud about our problems.

But what if we are the giver of advice? What then? If we have been in a similar situation or know someone who has, the best thing we can do is recount what they or we did and how it worked out.

It's always better to talk about things that we have experienced and have happened; it gives credence to what we are saying and is far more acceptable than something that starts with "This is what you should do".

Be cautious about telling people what they should do. They may go out and do it!

If you can tell the difference between good advice and bad advice, you don't need advice.

Laurence J. Peter

September 4

Others

Over every mountain, there is a path, although it may not be seen from the valley.

Theodore Roethke

There is us. And there are other people. The clue here is in the word other. It indicates that they are not us. And we want to let them get on with their lives. We want to stop interfering in their journey. They are different to us. They have their path, and we have ours.

Let us concentrate on our path and do our best to be magnificent. Or at least, alright. And stop trying to work out what, why, and how they will mess things up.

As soon as we think about them, we move into judgement mode. And we know that judgement is not good. So why are we doing it "again"?

Let's do love. Let's do our best. Be our best. Let's let them do whatever they need to do. It's their journey, and it's hard enough trying to get our journey right. Let's give ourselves a break. Let's just love ourselves and love them too.

If the path be beautiful, let us not ask where it leads.

Anatole France

September 5

Choice

My entire life, I have viewed every problem as an opportunity – I've had no choice.

Clara Shih

We are not locked into who we are. We do not have to continue to behave the way we do.

We do not have to accept the roles that other people give us.

Many people drift through their lives, accepting their lot without thought. They may moan or complain about it, but they never actually do anything to change it or themselves.

So many of us are taken advantage of by others and go along with this because it has never occurred to us that it could be any other way.

There is a difference between doing things because we choose to do them and doing them because we believe we have to do them. We have a choice. We are not enslaved. We want to learn how to choose what we do and have the self-respect to do it.

God always gives his best to those who leave the choice with him.

Jim Elliot

September 6

Self-pity

Self-pity in its early stage is as snug as a feather mattress.
Only when it hardens does it become uncomfortable.

Maya Angelou

Poor me... Emoji weeping face.
It's not fair...
Why...
Why me...
As we spiral down the rabbit hole
How pathetic.
And we know it.
But we just can't help it.

And even if you haven't succumbed to many of the above for ages, I cannot believe you are totally blameless.

It may be the lesser version, but here we go again...

And the more self-centred we are and the more we focus on ourselves, the worse it gets as it spirals down.

When we take our attention off ourselves, things improve. When we take our hearts out of the black hole and start helping others life opens up.

Also, bad things have happened to everyone, not just to you. Bad things and good things. It's called life. It undulates. The trick is to enjoy the moment you are in, however challenging it is...

Discontent, blaming, complaining, self-pity cannot serve as a foundation for a good future, no matter how much effort you make.

Eckhart Tolle

September 7

Cages

God loved the birds and invented trees, man loved the birds and invented cages.

Jacques Deval

Why would anyone cage a bird? What an appalling thing to do. Come to that, why would anyone have a zoo filled with caged animals?

Having something in your cage means that it has to follow your rules. You remove its freedom of choice. You dictate how it behaves.

Why would anyone choose to be caged? Why would they walk willingly into a relationship that will confine them?

Surely they cannot be stupid enough to think that it will all change. Surely they must have the sense to realise that it will only get worse as the rules and demands tighten.

And yet it is possible to walk to freedom. Every day we wait, makes the first step harder. We are meant to be alive and free.

Claim your freedom. Own it.

The truth is I love being alive. And I love feeling free. So if I can't have those things, then I feel like a caged animal, and I'd rather not be in a cage. I'd rather be dead. And it's real simple. And I think it's not uncommon.

Angelina Jolie

September 8

Change

The measure of intelligence is the ability to change.

Albert Einstein

Nothing stays the same. Everything is changing all the time. Very often, it does not feel as if this is true. We think we are stuck in a "forever" rut.

If things in our lives are good or bad, whether we feel empowered or useless, they will change.

Life is really like riding a horse. It will or won't jump over a fence. It finds it much harder going through the wet ploughed ground than across grass. Then it suddenly wants to drink or eat. And all the time, we are doing our best to stay on it.

There will be great joy and great pain. Accept it. Who you were, who you are, and who you are becoming is more than enough. Accept it.

Be grateful for the ride.

In riding a horse, we borrow freedom.

Helen Thompson

Love

The greatest weakness of most humans is their hesitancy to tell others how much they love them while they're alive.

Orlando A. Battista

My love keeps me alive.

No, my love makes my aliveness radiant. Totally flowing out of me, crescendo after crescendo. I spread my arms and fly. And that incandescent light, my love, glides on and out into the world.

That you exist and that I love you is overwhelming.

I'm shy and human, and sometimes I find it hard to put my feelings into words. Perhaps no words can begin to do justice to how I feel.

In the last couple of years of my mother's life, I attempted to tell her how much I loved her. It was difficult, nearly impossible, for both of us. In some way, it seemed that if we were to put our love into words, we would be admitting that she was going to die. So we didn't manage many good words. But we did a lot of good (and painful) feelings.

And so, back to the circle.

My love keeps me alive.

My love for you burns so brightly in me.

I am alive.

The pain of love is the pain of being alive. It's a perpetual wound.

Maureen Duffy

We are most alive when we're in love.

John Updike

Credit

Credit, where credit is due, is a very rewarding habit to form. Its rewards are inestimable.

Loretta Young

Most of us do not value ourselves highly enough, and we do not give ourselves the credit we deserve.

We almost certainly underestimate our abilities and talents. We are magnificent human beings. We want to pat ourselves on the back and delight in the goodness and light we bring into the world.

However, there are those who are "very important people" who trample their way through life. But even they generally suffer from self-doubt in some area of their life.

And it is worth mentioning that just because someone is "very successful" in one area of their life does not mean they are successful in all areas.

It is important to be a well-rounded person and to be able to give love to all the people we meet.

Do yourself a favour, pat yourself on the back now, and say, "Thank you" and "Well done".

You have to give yourself credit, not too much because that would be bragging.

Frank McCourt

Freedom

You wanna fly, you got to give up the shit that weighs you down.

Toni Morrison

The idea of living in freedom is appealing, surely. We are not talking about a country or the environment we live in. We're talking about everyday life.

So yes, if asked, the idea of freedom is appealing.

And yet ever since we were born, others have controlled us to a certain extent. And we also, as time has passed, started to manipulate others too. Our interactions with them have a set of rules, and whenever we obey their rules, or they obey ours, there is control. There is no true freedom.

And so, to be free, we want to let go of our demands and expectations about others.

We want to learn to walk, be, do, and experience the world with the freedom of being. Rather than obeying expectations because that is what we expect ourselves to do.

Choose.

Live.

Enjoy.

The unhappiest people in this world are those who care most about what other people think.

C. JoyBell C

September 12

Sharing

Most people talk too much, and what they do say is often just noise or irrelevant gibberish designed to keep themselves entertained.

Stuart Wilde

We all know people who will pour out all their troubles to anyone who is there, given a quarter of a chance. Regardless.

And it is therapeutic for them. (It may have gone from being therapeutic into some ghastly self-obsession, but that's another issue.)

It is therapeutic to tell someone what is happening in our lives. To share our troubles. To give our mind a spring clean.

If we don't, our troubles, our difficulties, call them what you will, tumble around in our heads, feeding on one another. They cause us pain. They affect us mentally and physically.

We want to talk about them, even if we do not find a solution in the talking. Identifying their different aspects will give us a degree of clarity.

Friends share all things.

Pythagoras

Troubles

*Of all your troubles, great and small, the greatest are the
ones that don't happen at all.*

Thomas Carlyle

And we think we've got troubles. Times when we are just
hanging on, or maybe just living through what seems like an
endless struggle. Often with little or no help. Even when
there is help, there is still no help.

I spoke to someone the other day, "It's been a terrible
year," he said, "I lost my driving license and both my
parents." (One may question the order of his troubles, but
one can see he's had a bad year. And they are probably more
significant than what we are facing.)

Then I heard a story about a man whose wife had only a
couple of weeks to live, he finally got her into a hospice. He
went home and died that same day. This may seem sad, but I
think it's gently heartwarming. He had done all he could for
his wife. He had fulfilled his commitment to her, so he could
go home, sit down and gently die because now he was able
to.

Let's save tomorrow's troubles for tomorrow.

Patricia Briggs

Intimacy

My great hope is to laugh as much as I cry; to get my work done and try and to love somebody and have the courage to accept the love in return.

Maya Angelou

Intimacy. What an enormous word. True intimacy is being totally open with someone else. Nothing hidden. Complete disclosure. The gift of oneself as one truly is. It is indescribably worthwhile, of course, we risk being rejected.

But the benefit, the joy we feel when we are accepted, far outweighs the possible distress of rejection.

Intimacy wants to be ongoing. Just because you confessed to stuff ten years ago certainly doesn't create intimacy today unless you are still doing it.

If fear is the greatest enemy of intimacy, love is its true friend.

Henri Nouwen

Intimacy is a totally different dimension. It is allowing the other to come into you, to see you as you see yourself.

Osho

September 15

Prayer

The gods either have power, or they have not. If they have not, why pray to them? If they have, then instead of praying to be granted or spared such and such a thing, why not rather pray to be delivered from dreading it, or lusting for it, or grieving over it? Clearly, if they can help man at all, they will help him in this way.

Marcus Aurelius

In the final analysis, things will or won't happen, and tomorrow, next week or next year, life will be going on, and whether it happens or not, will not be enormously important.

So...

Rather than praying for a lover, pray that you can be happy whether you have one or not.

Rather than praying for the job, the result you want, or for world peace, pray that you may be happy and able to get on with your life, regardless of the outcome.

Let go of your desires, let god deal with events, and move forward with peace and the ability to do whatever you can when the time comes.

Open your eyes, look within. Are you satisfied with the life you're living?

Bob Marley

September 16

Responsibility

The alcoholic is like a tornado roaring his way through the lives of others. We feel a man is unthinking when he says sobriety is enough. He is like the farmer who came up out of his cyclone cellar to find his home ruined. To his wife, he remarked, "Don't see anything the matter here, Ma. Ain't it grand the wind stopped blowin'?"

Alcoholics Anonymous

Even without being alcoholics, many of us cause devastation in our lives and the lives of everyone involved with us. We do things that damage everyone. And when we come out of it and get back on an even keel, we assume everything and everyone else is okay.

But more often than not, they continue to suffer for ages after. We broke the rules. We behaved in a way that they cannot understand.

And we want to apologise to them. Apologise with our whole being. Because somewhere in the back of their minds, lives fear. "Fear" that we will suddenly "go off the rails" again. Probably without any warning.

And so, it is essential that we find a way to reassure them that we are okay and demonstrate that we have changed. Saying "I'm sorry" and not changing is not being sorry.

Never ruin an apology with an excuse.

Benjamin Franklin

An apology is the superglue of life, it can repair just about anything.

Lynn Johnston

Pain

Bad things do happen; how I respond to them defines my character and the quality of my life. I can choose to sit in perpetual sadness, immobilised by the gravity of my loss, or I can choose to rise from the pain and treasure the most precious gift I have – life itself.

Walter Anderson

We cannot avoid pain. And if we did, we would be the loser because everything we experience is a lesson, good or bad. These are what make us whole. So we want to accept the pain that comes to us, however awful it is, because it gives us strength and wisdom.

Whenever we are suffering, if we stop for a moment, go into it, and say, "Thank you" to it, it changes and becomes easier to travel through.

It ceases to be an enormous insurmountable agony. It just becomes part of the series of events that mark our journey. It loses power when we thank it, and gives it perspective.

Take chances, make mistakes. That's how you grow. Pain nourishes your courage. You have to feel in order to practice being brave.

Mary Tyler Moore

Aggression

A lion shows his fangs, a man hides his.

Marty Rubin

You probably think of ducks as being gentle, good-natured animals. A good role model, perhaps.

And yet, as I watch them on the river, they constantly push each other out of the way. And I am reminded of a thing that happened about forty years ago. I was walking by one of the Hampstead ponds in London, where several mothers with children were feeding the ducks. A sparrow kept flitting in and grabbing tasty morsels. Then one of the ducks opened its beak and swallowed the sparrow whole. Its tail feathers sticking out of the corner of its mouth. The mothers and children screamed and ran away.

It's a funny world, isn't it? A lot more violence in it than we might guess. But at least the ducks don't go to war with one another.

If you want to release your aggression, get up and dance. That's what rock and roll is all about.

Chuck Berry

Loss

If you're not careful, you can spend your whole life looking for what you've lost.

Moira Fowley-Doyle

"Have you seen...?"

"Do you know where... is?"

Oh, the hours, if you add them all up, the time we've spent hunting for things. And yet we all know at least one person who always knows where everything is.

The difference between them and you is that when they put something down, they take a fraction of a second to notice where they put it.

They also have a place for things.

So much more fun.

Things are never lost to you; you are lost to them. If ever in need of a thing that has lost you, simply stop hiding from it.

Shannon Hale

September 20

Love

Beauty is how you feel inside, and it reflects in your eyes. It is not something physical.

Sophia Loren

And that is the case with love too. Love is how you feel inside and how they make you feel. It is not physical. It is our souls embracing each other. All the other stuff is just a distraction.

Our ego(s) trying to place limitations, expectations, judgement, satisfaction, desire, and "what will others think" and any other lie it can create to distort our love and keep us under control. It is very good at it. Very, very good. Such a pity. Allow your soul the freedom to love with freedom. Live.

Lovers don't finally meet somewhere. They're in each other all along.

Rumi

Important encounters are planned by the souls long before the bodies see each other.

Paulo Coelho

Attachments

If you realise that all things change, there is nothing you will try to hold onto. If you are not afraid of dying, there is nothing you cannot achieve.

Lao Tzu

Our attachment to things and people causes us pain and distress. We want things to last forever, and even though we know, if we think clearly about them, that they cannot last forever, we want them to. And we fear their ending. We fear being without.

And a lot of the time, we do it unconsciously. It is like a small grey cloud that we keep on the end of a string and pull along, so it's always hovering nearby.

Suppose we think about our home, partner, child, parent, job or favourite mug, and realise they will no longer be with us in due course.

If we do that with gentle wisdom, it begins our journey of freedom from them.

For the person who has learned to let go and let be, nothing can ever get in the way again.

Meister Eckhart

It's not much of a tail, but I'm sort of attached to it.

Eeyore – A. A. Milne

Awakening

We do not have a fear of the unknown. What we fear is giving up the known.

Anthony De Mello

How we hang on to the things in our comfort zone, bumbling along like sheep in a field with too much fresh green grass, which we continue to eat. Yes, we may push ourselves into new thoughts and behaviours, but less and less, as we get older, the comfort of the familiar calls to us.

And that isn't necessarily bad, but it is sad.

We might feel better about ourselves and our life if we took some risks. (Even a tiny little risk, like eating something different or going another way).

The thing about taking a risk is that we have to be alive to do it. Not just the living dead.

A thought is a screen, not a mirror; that is why you live in a thought envelope, untouched by reality.

Anthony De Mello

September 23

Criticism

You have been criticising yourself for years, and it hasn't worked. Try approving of yourself and see what happens.

Louise L. Hay

It is one of the things that most of us are masters or mistresses of. Self-criticism and self-putdowns. Affirmations of our failures and shortcomings. Reinforcing the behaviour each time we say or think it.

Oh, and most of us are good at drawing attention to, or at least making a mental note of, all the failures of others.

Please realise that I am not criticising you when I mention this. You are just suffering from the worldwide pandemic of criticism.

So now that we realise that...

We know that we can choose how we behave and how we react.

We know that.

We can start to look for opportunities to praise ourselves and others. We will change the world, very gently, quietly.

The more you praise and celebrate your life, the more there is in life to celebrate.

Oprah Winfrey

September 24

Teaching

You cannot teach a man anything, you can only help him find it within himself.

Galileo

We are teachers. Wherever we go, whoever we are with, we are teaching them, and they are teaching us.

The idea of being a teacher is foreign to many of us. But when we accept it, we are confronted with the question. "What am I teaching?" (We're not talking about maths or sports here, we're talking about living life.)

Any negative thought or action we indulge in (because it is an indulgence) spreads through our being and out into the people we meet.

We are teaching them about us and how they should interact with the world.

What a responsibility when you look at it like that!

So the question is, what do we really want to teach? What do we want to teach when we look into our inner being, our soul?

Peel away enough layers, and the answer is love. We want to give and receive love. So let's care about people, feel love, love for ourselves and the world and teach that.

I touch the future. I teach.

Christa McAuliffe

September 25

Boomerangs

All life is a boomerang. We receive what we give.

Shirley MacLaine

It all comes back to us. So it's all down to us.

When we judge others as being different from us, less intelligent, less thoughtful, less anything, we damage them and harm ourselves. It is easy to think of our boss or the people who work for us, or under us, as different. To filter our reactions to them in an "appropriate" way. It is also easy to think, "Oh, I don't do that," but are you sure?

If we decide to approach people positively, with interest and (even?) with love, our relationships will be much better. Our lives will be better. We will be better.

I forgot how to throw a boomerang, but then it came back to me.

Hank Green

Death

Life is hard. Then you die. Then they throw dirt in your face. Then the worms eat you. Be grateful it happens in that order.

David Gerrold

The idea is to die young as late as possible.

Ashley Montagu

If you woke up this morning and realised that in seven hours and twenty-seven minutes, you would be dead, what would you do?

Call someone?
Water your plants?
Go for a beautiful walk?
Sit down and wail?
Eat delicious food?
Make love?
Get all your family around to watch you?
Write a will?
Go to the hospital?

I could suggest for hours and not even touch on your list. But I recommend choosing one of the things on your list and doing it. Don't put off the important things for the mundane.

We're born alone, we live alone, we die alone. Only through our love and friendship can we create the illusion for the moment that we are not alone.

Orson Welles

Love

"What is love?" "The total absence of fear." said the Master.

"What is it we fear?" "Love." said the Master.

Anthony De Mello

Love, total being. The unquestioning completeness. The ultimate gift. The ability to give and receive without any questioning. Freedom.

Without freedom, it is not love. If there is a need, the need is a blockage to love. So no conditions, no demands, no expectations. Just love.

Your happiness is love. Your happiness is that they are happy, even if that makes you unhappy.

If you are unhappy, your unhappiness is created by your wants, demands, and expectations. As soon as you need them, you are no longer doing love. You are tiptoeing towards fear.

Love.

This is a journey without distance, stop travelling and you arrive.

Anthony De Mello

September 28

Growing up

We worry about what a child will become tomorrow, yet we forget that he is someone today.

Stacia Tauscher

Isn't it funny how day by day nothing changes, but when you look back, everything is different.

C. S. Lewis

Do you remember being a youth, knowing all the answers, and not wanting to listen? And the pain and the struggles we had to go through to learn...

And it was the learning that made us whole and who we are today.

And when we have our own children, we want to spare them the pain we went through. We want to help them not to make the same mistakes.

And one day they will remember being a youth and...

It's been going on for so long. We want to find some balance between teaching and restricting. Being overprotective is almost always more damaging than giving freedom.

Give freedom. Allow growth. Allow adventure. So important to do and discover for ourselves. So important.

Growing old is mandatory, growing up is optional.

Walt Disney

You don't stop laughing when you grow old, you grow old when you stop laughing.

George Bernard Shaw

September 29

Respect

The greatest thing in the world is to know how to belong to oneself.

Michel de Montaigne

How would you treat it if someone gave you or you won the most magnificent racehorse, guaranteed to win race after race?

Would you feed it junk food? Would you let it sit around watching mindless TV?

Would you disrespect it and let others treat it as an old mindless workhorse?

Respect yourself, and others will respect you.

Confucius

September 30

Attitude

Your attitude, not your aptitude, will determine your altitude.

Zig Ziglar

So we get up in the morning and arm ourselves for the day. Our attitude has wrapped itself around us and our expectations before it starts.

If you think about the people you know, some are happy and successful, while others seem to find everything a struggle. Things go wrong in their lives. The source is their attitude and expectation. If we choose to have a positive outlook, we get the good things. It is that simple. We get what we choose to expect.

You cannot control what happens to you, but you can control your attitude toward what happens to you, and in that, you will be mastering change rather than allowing it to master you.

Brian Tracy

Read

Enjoy

Share

Thinking

*Don't believe everything you think. Thoughts are just that –
thoughts.*

Allan Lokos

Endless thoughts. On and on. Get rid – no, sorry, move
on from one because it is still waiting to be recycled – and
the next one comes barging in.

And all that when we are alone.

But mix with people, and in a quiet moment, you find
yourself wondering about what they are thinking about you.
You're not even thinking about what the conversation is
about anymore.

Don't do it. Just be proud to be the incredible,
magnificent human being you are. Shine and share yourself
and your being and your words. Courage. Enjoy

*Your mind is working at its best when you're being
paranoid. You explore every avenue and possibility of your
situation at high speed with total clarity.*

Banksy

*To paraphrase several sages: Nobody can think and hit
someone at the same time.*

Susan Sontag

October 2

Love

If the heart doesn't love, it becomes homeless. If there is no love, then why do people live.

Omar Khayyam

When we are "in love", it seems impossible that anyone can ever have experienced what we are feeling.

Yes, the world is filled with songs, poems, and words of love, and we may use them to increase our feelings. But we still cannot believe that the authors can have ever felt the way we do.

As time passes and our flame lessens, we can keep it burning brightly forever if we choose to. But most people do not do that. They allow it to die and quietly move to tolerance (or worse).

Keep your flames burning.

Keep them burning.

Rejoice.

Enjoy.

Oh love, there is no other life – but here.

Omar Khayyam

If I don't enjoy myself now, when shall I?

Omar Khayyam

Carrying on

If you are distressed by anything external, the pain is not due to the thing itself, but to your estimate of it, and this you have the power to revoke at any moment.

Marcus Aurelius

We have the power to choose how we respond to everything.

Yes, when some major disaster happens, or someone we love dies or is injured, our natural reaction floods through us before we can blink. But what we do next is up to us.

Do we give in to the pain and become helpless, or do we get on and do what needs to be done?

And in a week or three, are we still wallowing in the blackness of despair, or are we allowing ourselves to be alive? To be the positive person that we are capable of being?

A British pilot called Douglas Bader lost his legs in an air crash. Despite this, he continued to fly and was a fighter pilot in the RAF during the second world war.

Somehow that puts our troubles into a different perspective.

A challenge only becomes an obstacle when you bow to it.

Ray Davis

Worry often gives a small thing a big shadow.

Swedish Proverb

Effects

There are things known and there are things unknown, and in between are the doors of perception.

Aldous Huxley

So many of us journeying through change and self-acceptance are doing it on our own. And even if we are fortunate enough to be sharing our journey with others, we are still alone. Nobody can honestly understand what we are going through.

It is very easy to view ourselves in isolation and think less of our achievements than they deserve.

Any change from negative to positive is vast. Yet we can easily not acknowledge it. We measure the change in ourselves, and when we do that, it often feels as if we have achieved far less than we have.

I was talking about this with a friend, and he pointed out that everything we do impacts not only ourselves but also our families and everyone we come into contact with.

And when I look at my journey from that perspective, it changes how I see it. I feel humbled and grateful that the things I do spread out into the world with far more significant effects than I imagined.

It makes me say, "Thank you" to myself, increasing my resolution to continue.

You cannot get through a single day without having an impact on the world around you. What you do makes a difference, and you have to decide what kind of difference you want to make.

Jane Goodall

Some people arrive and make such a beautiful impact on your life, you can barely remember what life was like without them.

Anna Taylor

Lift

my mother
is pure radiance
she is the sun
I can touch
and kiss
and hold
without
getting burnt.

Sanober Khan

My mom smiled at me. Her smile kind of hugged me.

R. J. Palacio

This is best done lying down in bed. But you can do it sitting too.

Completely settle into whatever is supporting your body. Relax into it.

Become aware that it is lifting you. Lifting you with love. It is like your mother's hands and arms as she lifted you when you were an infant.

Feel that love. Feel the security. Feel the hand that is lifting you with total unconditional love. Let the feeling flow throughout your body. Feel the joy and happiness that it fills you with.

Stay there for as long as you wish. Bring the love, power, and happiness with you into your day, into the world.

I realised when you look at your Mother, you are looking at the purest love you will ever know.

Mitch Albom

Love

*There is one pain, I often feel, which you will never know.
It's caused by the absence of you.*

Ashleigh Brilliant

Love is one of the things that can consume us. Almost to the extent that we can cease to function.

I am talking about being in love, the more head over heels, the better. When we are in love, we are filled with joy. But when we are in love and are not with the person we love, it is easy to be drawn into sadness and torment because we aren't with them and are worrying about what is happening to them.

We can be stabbed, pain crashing through us, so that we can end by being miserable most of the time.

To change that, when we think of them, think of our love and let a smile spread across our face as we feel the joy of our love filling us.

Love unlocks doors and opens windows that weren't even there before.

Mignon McLaughlin

Control

The primary symptom of a controller is denial, that is, I can't see its symptoms in myself.

Keith Miller

Are you a controller? Do you get other people to do what you want? Do you nearly always get your way?

"Who me?" "No, no, no, I'm not like that." "Well, maybe a little, sometimes, but it is all for the best. It's in their interests. I am not selfish."

Okay, okay, I believe you...

So here's a different question: "How often do you do what you don't want to do?" Think about that one.

If you are not doing things you don't want to do, you must be manipulating how things unfold to get the outcome you want.

It bears thinking about. Are you achieving things at the expense of others?

Until you realise how easy it is for your mind to be manipulated, you remain the puppet of someone else's game.

Evita Ochel

October 8

Searching

*Both what you are running away from and what you are
searching for is inside you.*

Anthony de Mello

Even if we do not think of ourselves as running away, if
we delve a little, we will see that there are things in our lives
that we are trying to avoid. We may not even be able to name
them, but we can feel their presence in our body.

And what are we searching for? What is it that we secretly
(or openly) want? What is it we crave that will make us feel
fulfilled? It is possible that you may not find it easy to put
that into words.

Perhaps it is recognition, love, acceptance, oneness, or
peace. Maybe a new car or a bigger house. But if it is an
object, what will that do for us? Or rather, what do we think
it will do for us?

The object is just a sop to quieten us for a few minutes or
days, but it will not fill our inner hole. We will be off looking
for the next thing we delude ourselves into thinking is the
answer.

So, as it says in the quote, the answer is inside us. That is
where we can have peace. Only there can we stop running
away or searching. Just accept that is the first step to
freedom.

*Why do you so earnestly seek the truth in distant places?
Look for delusion and truth in the bottom of your own
heart.*

Ryokan

Fear

Fears are nothing more than a state of mind.

Napoleon Hill

Fear of something is at the root of hate for others, and hate within eventually destroys the hater.

George Washington Carver

If we are struggling in any area of our lives, suffering from mental or physical pain, perceiving the world as tormented and riddled with troubles, the cause of this is fear.

And fear is so very contagious. Let's simplify that. If we are troubled by something, the reason it bothers us is fear. And we then grab the next thing we have a problem with and increase the fear in that, and so on it goes, like a forest fire roaring through our being.

We want to do the next easy thing to make it disappear. But it does not work because whatever we use, we are just addressing the symptoms, not the cause. And as we do that, the symptoms become the cause too.

We are like someone on a treadmill, running, running, running, out of breath, and totally exhausted, but the very idea of getting off the treadmill does not even occur to us. The only solution to fear, the only escape from fear, is love.

We have love inside our heart all the time. To go there is simple. When we do, fear disappears. We can, if we choose, go through our day with love.

Do you want to know a secret? Fear is not real.

Saskia Lightstar

If you know the secret of life. You too would choose no other companion but love.

Rumi

Self-image

Forgive yourself for not having the foresight to know what now seems so obvious in hindsight.

Judy Belmont

Sometimes, a feeling of being less than, almost worthless, floods us. Everyone we know is doing so well, and we, well, we... we can't even find a word to describe our feeling of uselessness. And even if we do not jump that deeply into the pit, we still struggle.

Some people have a lot of self-confidence and self-belief and can tick off an endless array of achievements and accolades, but even they feel the shafts of the self-doubt arrows as they thud into their bodies.

And, of course, the laughable part of it is that we are doing it to ourselves. We are the one who is creating and accepting the negative self-image that is dragging us down.

I remember walking down a passage to a meeting. I was fifteen minutes late and filled with fear, imagining everyone judging me, and thinking I was a failure. But just as I reached the door, I changed my mindset to confidence, I walked in, smiling and nodding to everyone, so I changed the reality of everyone in the room.

It is possible to discard a negative self-image and choose a confident one. We simply want to do it and enjoy our time here. It is much nicer for everyone else too.

You yourself, as much as anybody in the entire universe, deserve your love and affection.

Buddha

Nothing in life causes more pain and suffering than the judgements we hold about and against ourselves.

Iyanla Vanzant

Finishing

*You can be in the race, but unless you finish, one might say,
the race wasn't in you.*

Brent M. Jones

How many things in your life have you started and never finished?

The raw enthusiasm at the beginning of a project gradually diminishes until it is laid aside. If that doesn't sound familiar, then "Bravo!"

But most of us lose our enthusiasm, and the task becomes a bore, a duty, a drudge. And more often than not, it is because we never really committed to it. We never saw the finish line and the path that led there.

So it makes sense, should we want to change, to make a genuine commitment before we start. To realise what it will entail and resolve to do whatever it takes.

It does not mean non-stop action, but it does mean conscientiously working our way through to the end.

Enjoying the delight we will feel when it's finished enhances the process.

*Defeat doesn't finish a man, quit does. A man is not finished
when he's defeated. He's finished when he quits.*

Richard M. Nixon

October 12

Loneliness

*Where you used to be, there is a hole in the world, which I
find myself constantly walking around in the daytime, and
falling in at night. I miss you like hell.*

Edna St Vincent Millay

Loneliness.

That silent part (or not so silent part) travels with us
wherever we go, just plucking at the edge of our clothing. We
can go for ages without even being aware of it, but it is there.

And if we think about it at all, we imagine that it has to do
with having other people in our lives. Doing, loving, and
being with others.

But, of course other people have nothing to do with it. We
know that other people cannot make us angry, happy, or
pensive. We do the feelings to ourselves. And we can choose
not to do angry, happy or anything else. So we must, at some
level, be doing loneliness to ourselves.

If you go into loneliness, if you take a moment of stillness
to go into it, you will discover an infant inside you that is
loneliness. It has always been there, its tiny arms
outstretched, longing for, hoping for love, hugs, and
acknowledgement.

If you take a little more time of peace and love to hold
and cherish the infant crying inside you, your loneliness will
fade into love.

The loneliness will float away, leaving you whole and at
peace.

*Pray that your loneliness may spur you into finding
something to live for, great enough to die for.*

Dag Hammarskjold

Distress

You pray in your distress and in your need; would that you might pray also in the fullness of your joy and in your days of abundance.

Khalil Gibran

We are never devoid of distresses; our peace of mind depends on our heart's way of accepting the strife.

Munia Khan

Even if your times of distress and pain are a distant memory, and I hope they are, we have all suffered them to a greater or lesser extent.

When we are in them, truly down and dirty, overwhelmed by everything, it seems there can be no way out.

We are such failures, useless, worthless, and totally undeserving. It is all so utterly dreadful.

And when someone we know is suffering, their agony tearing at our heart, we feel so inept and useless.

Somehow that old friend "This too shall pass" seems inadequate.

But at our core, we know that it will pass. We just have to ride it out or be there with them while they do.

We know there have been black times before; they passed, and this one will too.

The more you practice tolerating uncomfortable emotions, the more confident you'll become in your ability to tolerate the distress that may be necessary to reach your full potential.

Amy Morin

Responsibility

Never complain, never explain.

Benjamin Disraeli

That's it.
Live by that.
No more f-ing about.
Just get on with your life.
Choose to be true to yourself.
Don't hide behind a load of rubbish.
Don't point your finger at anyone.
Don't point your finger at yourself.
If you don't like what's happening or what you're doing, change it.
I know it is not as easy as clapping our hands, but it is good for us to take the odd look at ourselves and consider our life.

The buck stops here.

Harry S. Truman

I love working for myself; it's so empowering. Except when I call in sick. I always know I'm lying.

Rita Rudner

October 15

Peace

This day I choose to spend in perfect peace.

Gerald G. Jampolsky

Wow, what a quote. What an intention. Just reading, "This day I choose to spend in perfect peace", I can feel my head changing. And my body. And my being. All are saying, "Oh yes, Oh yes."

Then my ego whispers, "Okay, have your few seconds of fun. I'm waiting. I'll get you. Don't worry."

So I reread the quote and feel the peace travelling through my body.

But yes, I know that "life" will return and get in the way. I am, after all, just a human being.

But if I set my intention now to have perfect peace. If I breathe that in, I may manage to have a lot of perfect harmony during the day.

Oh, so lovely.

Quite the best.

Start each day in my peace and stillness, then you can go forth and face whatever the day may bring in perfect peace and joy.

Eileen Caddy

He enjoys perfect peace, that peace beyond all understanding, which comes to its maximum only to the man who has given up golf.

P. G. Wodehouse

October 16

Receiving

*Don't judge each day by the harvest you reap, but by the
seeds you plant.*

Robert Louis Stevenson

Every day, we send messages out into the world, telling it
how it should be.

Every time we frown, ignore, don't listen, or complain,
every time we sigh or slump, the world, and the people in it,
lap it up and reinforce this reality.

Similarly, every time we smile, give attention, care and
love, we are repaid with the same and more.

So we influence, we create the world we exist in. All we
want to do is choose what kind of world we want, and do
more of the things we want in it.

So simple, even when it's hard for any reason.

*If you don't like what you are reaping, you had better
change what you have been sowing.*

Jim Rohn

Perception

*As he mused about these things, he realised that he had to
choose between thinking of himself as a poor victim of a
thief and as an adventurer in quest of his treasure.*

Paulo Coelho

Who's driving your brain? Who gets to choose which
road to take and what the scenery is? Who's the person who
leaps out of the car and interacts with the world?

Most people would not even consider that they had a
choice. They believe things are just the way they are, and
they can do little or nothing about it.

But, of course that's not the case. We create our world.
And our driver is either our ego or our inner being. Our ego
is the creator of fear and attack. Our inner being creates love
and peace.

We can decide who drives today. Now. This instant. And
we can choose the next and the next.

What world do you want to live in?

Life is a song, and the difference you make is the lyrics.

Michael Bassey Johnson

Choose well. Your choice is brief, and yet endless.

Goethe

Gratitude

It is a good day to be grateful
There is so much to be grateful for.

Astrid Brinck

It is an excellent day to be grateful, and there is so much to be thankful for.

The sky. The sun. The clouds. The rain. The next leaf you see. Your hand. Your breath. Your heart. Your smile.

So much.

So very much.

Gratitude is not words.

Gratitude is a feeling that fills you.

Swells through your being.

Overwhelms you.

Do it.

Be overwhelmed.

There is so much to be grateful for, one day at a time.

When eating fruit, remember the one who planted the tree.

Vietnamese Proverb

October 19

Harvesting

Don't judge each day by the harvest you reap, but by the seeds that you plant.

Robert Louis Stevenson

So hard to do, especially when we live in a world where instant gratification is the norm.

No rumination for us. Switch on the TV, the games console, the phone, and we get that false feeling of peace because our brain doesn't have to do anything.

When we are involved in any long-term project, we are champing for instant success and results. And it is easy to give up because we are not getting them. We think we are failing.

Not enough people are buying our product. We are not improving in the sport of our choice fast enough. Our children are not... We are not... (Fill in the blanks)

If we are clever enough to stop and continue to plant the seeds with love and gentle energy, we will be amazed by our achievements.

With every deed, you are sowing a seed, though the harvest you may not see.

Ella Wheeler Wilcox

Letting go

When I let go of what I am, I become what I might be. When I let go of what I have, I receive what I need.

Tao Te Ching

At times, quite often in the night, our ego is like an insane child at a kid's party. High on sugar, roaring around, pushing, fighting and bullying anyone who gets in its way. We scream, Stop! And it just charges on, heading for the most fragile and valuable thing in the room.

When our ego becomes a tornado, it's not easy to stop it, but it isn't impossible. Nothing is impossible. We know there have been times when it seemed overwhelming, but it did change. If that happened before, it can happen this time.

The first step towards quietening it down is to say "No" or "I'm not going to think about that anymore" and take a really slow, conscious breath. Completely mentally absorbing ourselves in the breath and concentrating on it.

The ego, plucky little chap, will almost certainly squirm its way back into our mind, with some new terror, before we have finished the breath.

But if we persist, "Is there anything I can do about this right now? At this moment?" and if there is not, then "I'm not going to think about this now." And another breath.

It is also good to move, and change your body. If you're in bed, get up, go to the bathroom, and have a glass of water. Look at something, really look at it. Another conscious breath. Another.

Visualise the thought dissolving and floating away. Breathe. Concentrate on the bedding touching your body. Relax your body one bit at a time. Become aware of each part. Know that this will all become a memory.

It is important that we forgive ourselves for making mistakes. We need to learn from our errors and move on.

Steve Maraboli

Parents

In some sense, every parent does love their children. But some parents are too broken to love them well.

William P. Young

To understand your parents' love, you must raise children yourself.

Chinese proverb

It is difficult to change our relationship with our parents or children into friendship. We tend to be locked into our authority or obedient or disobedient roles.

If you think about your relationship with your best friend, it is one of acceptance. It is not judgemental. It is open uninhibited and equal.

There are no secrets. It is based on unconditional love, with no expectations or demands.

Maybe there are other things that you can add to the list that make your relationship with your best friend special.

So if you want to move toward that with your parents or children, you want to talk to them about it and slowly allow yourself to open some of the doors you have kept closed. Discard some of the roles you have both played.

It is not easy, but it is truly wonderful if you can achieve it.

There are only two lasting bequests we can hope to give our children. One of these is roots, the other wings.

Hodding Carter

Judgement

It is the property of fools to be always judging.

Thomas Fuller

I knew a man who told me that he had a black notebook. Whenever anyone he knew or worked with did anything wrong (anything he disapproved of), he would jot it down in his notebook and score it one to ten. When anyone reached one hundred, he would cast them out of his life.

I found this extraordinary, and I told him so. I imagine I incurred at least a ten for this or even more.

I suggested that he throw the book away, and if he must have a book, he should have a red or multicoloured one.

If he must write things in a book, he wants only to write good or positive things. And when they reached one hundred, buy them a present.

I saw him about three years later, and I hardly recognised him. He radiated, beamed, and waved his red book at me, and if I were poetic, I would say that sparks or tiny angels flew upwards from the waving pages.

If you judge people you have no time to love them.

Mother Teresa

Moods

A change in the weather is sufficient to recreate the world and ourselves.

Marcel Proust

It has been cloudy for several days now, no rain, just clouds. It has been like that for so long that somehow I cannot imagine it not being cloudy.

When I was young and looked at the weather, I felt that the weather, whatever it was, must be like that all over the world. And although I know that wasn't true, it wasn't easy to imagine it not being like that.

We do that with our moods too. If we feel down, we view the world with the expectation that everyone else is down.

And to a certain extent, that is true because how we present ourselves to others is infectious. They tend to move emotionally towards our feeling.

So if we want to experience our lives as happy, then we want to do happiness as we go through our day. I say "do happiness" because we do our emotions. And if we don't feel the way we want, we can pretend, we can fake it, till we make it.

Wherever you go, no matter what the weather, always bring your own sunshine.

Anthony J. D'Angelo

Self-awareness

Who I was, who I am, and who I am becoming is more than enough.

Liza Colpa

So often, we are dissatisfied with ourselves. We carry the feeling of failure or lack of achievement somewhere in the back of our minds. It is an unqualified negative judgement of ourselves.

And, looking at it like that, there is nothing we can do about it because even if we do 'X' and it is magnificent, all our other named or unnamed shortcomings are waiting to drag us down again.

However, if we gently accept Liza's affirmation, without struggle or violent action, we can quietly begin to accept ourselves. Our existence with no expectations is enough.

You are imperfect, permanently and inevitably flawed. And you are beautiful.

Amy Bloom

There are people who make things happen, there are people who watch things happening, and there are people who wonder what happened.

Jim Lovell

Illness

*Never let the things you cannot do prevent you from doing
the things you can.*

Coach John Wooden

It's so unbelievably awful when someone you love is kneeling in front of a toilet, their head in the bowl, as they throw up, their body heaving with the effort.

It is ghastly when the one we love is ill, wracked with pain, and there is nothing we can do.

We feel so tiny, inept, pathetic, and long to help. How we wish there were something, anything that we could do. We feel isolated from the world, as if no one else has ever experienced the pain we feel at that moment. There are no words we can say to them that are of any help, except perhaps "I love you."

And if we say and feel that love, growing in us and spreading to them, we can move from the feeling of uselessness into the feeling of love. We can allow our love to expand and fill our mind and body. We can find peace in our love, and then nothing else matters. Love is all-encompassing.

*You can't calm the storm, so stop trying. What you can do is
calm yourself. The storm will pass.*

Timber Hawkeye

Connections

First child; 'Are you related to anyone famous?"

Second child; 'I don't want to brag, but I heard Dad calling god his father.

A child of god

Well, now you know, the cat's out of the bag. I didn't mean to tell you. But there it is, I am the son of God.

And I have countless brothers and sisters.

The trouble is that sometimes I forget this and treat you as ordinary. Sometimes even judging and looking down on you.

I hope that is just part of being human. I am striving to do better. Please forgive me and have patience.

I love mankind... It's people I can't stand.

Charlie Brown. Charles M. Schulz

Everyone is God speaking.

Why not be polite and listen to him.

Hafiz

October 27

Joy

The soul's joy lies in doing.

P. B. Shelley

Here's a challenge for you.

Do what you are doing with joy.

At the moment, you're reading. Do it with joy.

Feelings are done in the body, not in the mind. So in order to read this with joy, you will be feeling joy in your body. And now, the next thing you do, do it with joy. The way your hand moves, the weight of your foot on the ground, the air filling your chest.

Do each of them with joy.

And now see if you can do ten things in a row, one after the other, with joy. It is not easy, but it is fun.

And as you go through your day, remember to experience joy as you do something.

We cannot cure the world of sorrows, but we can choose to live in joy.

Joseph Campbell

Beliefs

A casual stroll through the lunatic asylum shows that faith does not prove anything.

Friedrich Nietzsche

What is the one statement anyone could make to you, that would stop you dead?

What is the one question, if you were asked, that would make you withdraw completely?

Is it the question or the answer that would disturb you at a core level?

What matters here is whether your reaction to the statement or question has more to do with others hearing it, or your own limiting beliefs.

Do your views, attitudes, and beliefs hold you hostage in a world you dislike?

You are not supposed to talk about three things: politics, religion, and money.

Although I came across this list of things, you should never talk about.

How you slept (no one cares)

Your ailments

Your journey

Your dreams

Money

Diets

The best ways to get from A to B

In fact, nobody cares about any of this stuff, so shut up.

And finally, if you want to be able to talk freely about anything, you should perhaps choose the person you're going to unload onto carefully.

It's discouraging to make a mistake, but it's humiliating when you find out you're so unimportant that nobody noticed it.

Chuck Daly

Work

Work without love is slavery.

Mother Teresa

The primary source of complaint in most people's lives is their job, their work, and the faults they find in it.

And yet it is the thing that occupies the bulk of our life. It is the thing, or should be the thing, that gives meaning to our existence.

Given our circumstances, it may be hard for many of us, but earning less, while filled with joy, can be magnificent.

In my twenties, I worked in the city, earning lots of money and hated every minute. I finally dared to leave and go and work in the theatre for a pittance. It was the best thing I ever did. It opened the doorway to life.

Choose a job you love and you will never have to work a day in your life.

Confucius

Learning

Everybody is a genius. But if you judge a fish by its ability to climb a tree, it will live its whole life believing it is stupid.

Albert Einstein

The world is our classroom. All the people we spend time with are our teachers. The events are lessons. We move through them onto the next event, the next lesson. Everything happens for a reason.

This is true of the good, the bad and even the ugly. It is all meant. It all passes. The lessons are repeated until we learn what we need from them.

Realising this alters our perspective on everything we do. It makes it easier. It gives our life space.

Questions are for the benefit of every student, not just the one raising his hand.

Ann Pratchett

Defects

Children are excellent observers, and will often perceive your slightest defects. In general, those who govern children, forgive nothing in them, but everything in themselves.

Francois Fenelon

Other people's character defects are such a rich source of negativity. We delight in finding ways to be critical of them and sometimes even imagine suitable punishments we think they should endure.

The truth is that we have not found a way to forgive ourselves for all the areas in our life where we have failed. We have yet to live up to the impossibly perfect person we think we should be.

(We know the truth about ourselves, and we also know the secrets that we hide. Ssh... Ssh... don't even whisper them.)

We want to forgive ourselves. We want to learn to accept and love ourselves. When we do that, we will find that our judgement falls away.

Because what we hate most in others are the things we hate most in ourselves.

It is only imperfection that complains of what is imperfect. The more perfect we are, the more gentle and quiet we become towards the defects of others.

Joseph Addison

If not

you...

who?

Ego

The ego is a demanding force that's never satisfied: It constantly requires that we seek more money, power, acquisitions, glory and prestige to provide the fuel it thinks it must have.

Wayne Dyer

Surely anyone reading that, realising that is what their ego is pursuing, would recognise the folly, the insanity of such a way to live.

And so, stopping everything for a few seconds and taking stock of our life... allowing this idea to settle in... what then?

In all honesty, we would ponder it for a few seconds and then go on with our lives unchanged. Hurrying on to the next bit of insanity. Maybe if we stop a few seconds longer and access the peace within us...

And then... what then?

The guard walks through the train, crying, "All change, all change", but we do not want to leave the comfort and warmth of our seat. Leave me in peace. Let me get on with my life, don't make me get off the train. If we wait, maybe another guard will come along, saying, "There's no need to change", and I can stay on this train, no need to change! Thank God for that.

To some people, the ego is evil. It gives you so much. It gives you everything you want. But it takes back too much in return. It gives you everything: money, riches, women, glamour, everything you want. But in return, it takes back so much, and you're soulless. That's its goal. The ego's goal is to leave you soulless.

Mike Tyson

Deciding

All our final decisions are made in a state of mind that is not going to last.

Marcel Proust

In fact, all our decisions, not just our final ones, are made in a state of mind that will change.

And that seems, both important, and not a thing that we consider when we make decisions or think about our opinions.

At the time, we feel so locked into them and their rightness, the very idea that we might ever think otherwise seems impossible.

And yet we change massively as we make our way through life. Our beliefs and our view of how things should be done also change.

So, we may get more out of life by realising we want to be open to the possibility that what we think today might be different by the time next year arrives.

If you can't change your mind, then you're not using it.

Bashar

Persecution

We are each our own devil and we make this world our hell.

Oscar Wilde

We persecute ourselves.

We are the judge, the jailor, and the hangman all rolled into one. We watch and laugh at our pain as it finds ways to cut more deeply.

And often, we continue doing things that hurt us the most.

Why?

What now?

If we are going to continue doing something, accept that this is our choice.

Continue, and allow ourselves to do it.

If we are going to stop, then stop.

Know that we have stopped and forgive ourselves for the past. It is gone.

Of course, if we say we aren't going to do something, and continue to do it, that is a shortcut to hell.

It comes to this then: there always have been people like me and always will be, and generally they have been persecuted.

E. M. Forster

November 4

Promises

The key to growth is to learn to make promises and to keep them.

Stephen R. Covey

Promises to ourselves or others.

Are the casual remarks, "Yes, I'll do that..." promises?

We probably don't think of them as promises. They may not even register as more than a noise floating through our head like a bird seen or perhaps sensed as we walk through the forest. We are not sure if it was a bird or if we imagined it. It's not there now, and that is obvious.

And when the casual thought or remark is to ourselves? That is even worse, more appalling, surely. "I must stop doing..." and then on we go, not even noticing that we've done it again.

What to do?

Anything?

Nothing?

Or start respecting ourselves?

Promises are worse than lies. You don't just make them believe, you make them hope.

Marilyn Monroe

Change

There are plenty of difficult obstacles in your path. Don't allow yourself to become one of them.

Ralph Marston

Change takes a long time. No, that's not true. All the things we do and avoid doing and all the pain we inflict on ourselves, takes a long time.

So ghastly. So much suffering. So much unnecessary pain. Although perhaps it isn't unnecessary, maybe it is essential.

We cannot, and we will not change until we are ready. There are no half-measures.

We shuffle towards the edge of the cliff. No, shuffle is wrong, we fight violently, doing everything we can not to reach the edge, breaking our fingernails as we cling to the cracks in the road. Until we do reach the edge and finally decide to step off.

Then one of two things happens, we fall and crash broken on the rocks because we have not truly let go. We are still at the top of the cliff fighting everything and everyone, including ourselves, to prevent change.

Or we fall, discover that we are a bird, and soar to freedom.

We have to let go completely to change, no ifs or buts, no maybes. No more trying to control it. Just surrender. Then it is easy. We are the flying bird.

And there is a slight chance that we may find it easier to step off by realising this.

Go on, the view is beautiful here.

If it is important to you, you will find a way. If not, you'll find an excuse.

Ryan Blair

Heart

Follow your heart, listen to your inner voice, stop caring about what others think.

Roy T. Bennett

Are you, right now, thinking, acting, and talking with your heart? Being in a position of love?

Or is it your mind, your ego, creating your world and influencing everything in it?

It is possible to spend more and more of our life manifesting peace and love in ourselves and all around us.

Be in your heart.

Operate from your heart.

It makes an unbelievable difference to your existence and everyone you are in contact with.

It changes everything.

Normality is a paved road. It's comfortable to walk, but no flowers grow on it.

Vincent Van Gogh

November 7

Insecurity

The task we must set for ourselves is not to feel secure, but to be able to tolerate insecurity.

Erich Fromm

When we recognise and accept that we suffer from insecurity, we are on the first step to overcoming it. So many of us blag our way through our day and life, pretending that we are okay.

But deep within us lies insecurity.

Deep within us also lies peace and love.

We can choose which one we embrace.

There is no meaning to life except the meaning man gives his life by the unfolding of his powers.

Erich Fromm

Pain

Without effort and willingness to experience pain and anxiety, nobody grows, in fact nobody achieves anything worth achieving.

Erich Fromm

So, there you have it. We have to go through pain to become and move on.

No pain. No gain.

And yet we shy away from it, roaring into reverse as soon as it appears.

Of course, we do.

Could we learn to dive into it and grow through it gracefully? It is certainly worth considering.

Man's main task in life is to give birth to himself, to become what he potentially is. The most important product of his effort is his own personality.

Erich Fromm

Punishing

Distrust all in whom the impulse to punish is powerful.

Friedrich Nietzsche

I'm human.

Sometimes people do things that get up my nose.

I want to retaliate. I want to get my own back. I want to punish them. Sometimes I even quite like the idea of humiliating them.

I start to rehearse the things that I shall say to them.

I see them shrivelling up in my mind's eye as my brilliantly chosen words utterly destroy them.

(Maybe you never do anything like that. If so, "Bravo"! Live joyfully with God.)

However, such a good word, "However", announces change elegantly.

However, at some stage, I remember that the only person I am hurting with my anger is myself. Attacking them will only add fuel to the pain I am inflicting upon myself.

And so, (often reluctantly), I take a deep breath and let go. I watch, with sorrow, my marvellously destructive words floating away into the ether.

I smile. Smile at myself with love. I let that love and smile grow. I haul an image of the other person into the love. I forgive them. (After all, it's not their fault that they are stupid.) I forgive myself for thinking that. I go back to the love, the forgiving them, forgiving me, and I let go. Bravo.

To forgive is to set a prisoner free and discover that the prisoner was you.

Lewis B. Smedes

The weak can never forgive. Forgiveness is the attribute of the strong.

Mahatma Gandhi

Puppy

I think dogs are the most amazing creatures, they give unconditional love. For me, they are the role model for being alive.

Gilda Radner

I'm getting a puppy next week.

To keep me young.

To share love with.

I should know what to expect. I've had puppies before. And babies. But I have forgotten what it is like.

I move through the house, tidying and picking up more things. Will she chew through the electric wires, I wonder. Not often, I think.

So good (I hope) to be starting a new adventure. No, it is "So good to be starting a new adventure."

It is vital to do things that challenge us, make demands on us, and keep us on our toes.

Dog is God spelt backwards.

Duane Chapman

Words

There is no try, there is only do.

John Green

I'm not trying to be sexy, it's just my way of expressing myself when I move around.

Elvis Presley

Let's clean up our language. Our unconscious listens to everything we say and uses that to create our reality. And there are several words that we want to banish from our lives forever.

The first is "try" every time we say we are going to try to do something, it's a message to our unconscious to fail. You only have to think of all the times you've said you would "try to do something..." to know this is true.

From now on, say, "I will do that", or just as good, "No I won't do it."

The next word is "can't" every time we say we can't, we are absolving our responsibility. Change it to "choose not" to do something. Then we are taking control of our life.

And lastly, all the authority words our teachers and parents used, which cause us to rebel, words such as "must, have to, need to, ought to, got to, should." And when we use these on others, they rebel too. Change all of them, change them all to "want."

"You want to look good, don't you?" Enjoy!

We are living out the drama of a pathetic story, whose pages are smeared with our own handwriting.

Craig D. Lounsbrough

November 12

Freedom

There is freedom in stepping out and taking risks when you know at any given moment, you can always begin again.

Eva Gregory

Beginning again is not failure. It's freedom. It is a freedom that many of us fail to grasp. And starting again can be anything in our lives, from the tiny, deciding to take the cup into the kitchen, to the unimaginably vast, like leaving your home and moving abroad.

We so easily get trapped into things being the way they are.

Things are not the way we are. We allow them to be because we do not make an effort or decide to change them.

We are free. Or rather, we can be free whenever we choose to start being free.

Start before you're ready. Don't prepare, begin.

Mel Robbins

November 13

Adventure

If it feels right, give it a twirl.

Michael Ganly

Is that the same as 'if it doesn't feel wrong, give it a twirl?' Probably not completely. But how often do we hesitate before we take the plunge? Let's look at a simple example. How often do we try something that we never had before when eating out?

How often do we go the way we know when going for a walk? There is nothing wrong with staying with what we know.

But all the time, always, how sad. Let's go out there and give it a twirl.

If we were meant to stay in one place, we'd have roots instead of feet.

Rachel Wolchin

Forgiveness

Mistakes are always forgivable if one has the courage to admit them.

Bruce Lee

I can forgive, but I cannot forget, which surely means I will not forgive. I am hanging on to what happened.

If we peel away the layers of that statement, it means, I am still poisoning myself by holding on to it.

When we genuinely forgive, we forgive them totally, and we let go completely.

True forgiveness is not for their benefit, though hopefully, they will benefit. Genuine forgiveness is for our benefit. We are freed. We are released to live without the poison.

To forgive is to set a prisoner free and discover that the prisoner was you.

Lewis B. Smedes

Swans

*Millions of years ago, in my previous incarnations, I must
have been related to swans... Because I can still feel that
affinity.*

Jean Sibelius

On the river outside my window, there is a family of
swans, two parents and two nearly full-grown cygnets.

And then a couple of days ago, one of the cygnets
disappeared. I could feel the pain. What on earth kills
swans?

Apparently, foxes bite their heads off.

This is too awful.

And then yesterday. Spoiler alert it gets worse. Yesterday
there was only one swan and one cygnet.

I had the feeling of uselessness that one experiences when
you see a motorcycle flying through the air, with its rider
flying close by, and how the brain turns that into a slow-
motion event. Extraordinary.

I sat at my desk, bereft.

And then today the mother, father and two cygnets were
back again. How can that be? Other families?

But the one parent and one cygnet, something's wrong
there. The wind has just puffed, and the sunlight caught the
leaves falling from the oak tree. Isn't life wonderful.

Some people walk in the rain, others just get wet.

Roger Miller

On earth there is no heaven, but there are pieces of it.

Jules Renard

November 16

Magic

The world is full of magic things, patiently waiting for our senses to grow sharper.

W. B. Yeats

The world is full of magic. The way the light falls. The five birds flying by. The sound of your breathing. The thought in your mind. The stillness in your body. Your love for someone, someone's love for you, caring, compassion.

So much magic. So many miracles. How many can you experience, now and today? How often can you pull all of this wonder and brilliance into you today? How often can you let your wonder and joy at being alive embrace someone else's mind?

How many times can you stop being on autopilot, engrossed in a cloud of nothingness, and choose to be awake and alive?

Believe in your heart that you're meant to live a life full of passion, purpose, magic and miracles.

Roy T. Bennett

Being

One who knows more, loves more.

Catherine of Siena

If you are "now" what you should be... then what you've done in the past is irrelevant. What will light the fire and set the world blazing is what you do now. And the next now. And the now beyond that.

What matters is what we do, what we are thinking, saying, and feeling now.

Everything we do affects the world we perceive.

When we act with love and allow ourselves to be enveloped in love, the whole world, including us, benefits.

When we choose to follow, be led by, to travel with the inner voice of love, life is good.

Turn over the rudder in God's name and sail with the wind heaven sends us.

Catherine of Siena

To a brave man, good and bad luck are like his left and right hand. He uses both.

Catherine of Siena

Addiction

If a child had another disease, we'd be open about what we were going through, but addiction is stigmatised and comes with shame and guilt.

David Sheff

We all know the horror of the drug addict and alcoholic, and we may even pity them while they are locked into their illnesses.

But there are so many addictions. So many different ways we can succumb to addiction in one way or another.

Food, coffee, tea, and tobacco, to name some obvious ones. But how about TV, gaming, our phone, social media, or even checking our emails and text? The need for instant gratification overwhelms us, and we reach for them, disregarding life and living so we can lose ourselves elsewhere.

The solution?

The first step to a solution must be awareness and a desire to have more control over ourselves.

Without admitting our addiction, we cannot move on from it.

Unfortunately, with addiction, there's manipulation and deception.

Jeremy Camp

Habit

Sow an act, and you reap a habit. Sow a habit, and you reap a character. Sow a character, and you reap a destiny.

Charles Reade

It's so easy to get "out of the habit" of doing the good and important things in our lives. It is so hard to get "out of the habit" of doing the bad things we inflict upon ourselves.

Strange.

We stop doing the good things because our routine is disturbed somehow, so we don't do it today or this week. And then next week comes and... well, I'm busy, and I'm doing okay without doing it... and suddenly, it's gone. No longer in our life.

We do the bad things with little resistance. I'm not going to do it today. Oh well, okay, just once. Oh well, okay, I've started, so I will go on. There is no real battle because we have not decided to change.

An actual decision, an unbreakable contract with ourselves, is often helped by being witnessed by another.

So we make the change. We keep up our new behaviour for days, weeks...

And now our ego is just waiting for an opportunity to trip us up, and get us to revert, just once. Just this once, understand. Understand. It'll be okay. Don't worry. It will be okay, just this once.

Quietly is not an act, it is a habit.

Aristotle

The chains of habit are too weak to be felt until they are too strong to be broken.

Samuel Johnson

Want

When you can't have what you want, it's time to start wanting what you have.

Kathleen Sutton

So many of us want things. Want. Want. Want. It is endless.

Really, we want peace of mind, a feeling of completeness and freedom to exist as we want to. The only way we can ever achieve this is to enjoy what we have. To focus our delight on our present existence.

Then we can be complete, happy and free.

Remember that sometimes not getting what you want is a wonderful stroke of luck.

Dalai Lama

November 21

Openness

The most difficult subjects can be explained to the most slow-witted man if he has not formed any idea of them already; but the simplest thing cannot be made clear to the most intelligent man if he is firmly persuaded that he knows already, without a shadow of doubt what is laid before him.

Leo Tolstoy

It is so easy to close our minds to things. To shut out the possibility of another way to see things.

And even if we are open-minded, there are probably still some beliefs that we cling to as being unchangeable truths.

Perhaps we want to wonder about that.

In the midst of winter, I find within me the invisible summer.

Leo Tolstoy

The kingdom of God is within you.

Leo Tolstoy

Mind

You have two choices: to control your mind, or let your mind control you.

Paulo Coelho

What in your life do you have control over? Where you live and work? Your children, partner or parents? The government, the refuse collectors, public transport? What you eat? How you exercise or don't? How you worship?

In truth, the only thing we have control over is our mind, and how we use it. How we choose to view things, whether we approach a situation with love or fear.

The only thing we control is our mind, and most people don't bother to exercise any control over that. They allow themselves to be swept along, doing and believing whatever the latest piece of nonsense is that floats or crashes its way in.

It's your mind.

It's your choice.

What you do or don't do with it makes a difference.

If you don't control your mind, someone else will.

John Allston

November 23

Anger

Do not let the behaviour of others destroy your inner peace.

Dalia Lama

Anger is so damaging.

It is damaging to us. We cannot and do not operate properly or think clearly when we are angry.

You see professional sportspeople doing and saying things to make their opponents angry because they know that anger will reduce their abilities.

So, if we do anger, it makes sense now to feel the calmness that resides within us. To go into the peace and allow it to spread through us. And go on with the day, choosing to embrace the calm throughout the day.

If we slip back into anger, all is not lost. We can choose to stop and reconnect to calmness. And we want to have some slots in our life for meditation. Just a few minutes makes such an incredible difference to our well-being.

Where there is anger, there is always pain underneath.

Eckhart Tolle

November 24

Feeling Good

If you're happy, if you're feeling good, then nothing else matters.

Robin Wright

Let's be honest
We want to feel good about ourselves.

Yes, there may be people and things in our lives that we care passionately about or even love unconditionally. Still, we want to feel good about ourselves at the honest deepest level.

That is how we are.

You may now be disagreeing, challenging, or searching to prove that this isn't true. I respect that. I feel that too.

However, play with me here. Allow yourself the freedom, just for a fraction of a second, to entertain the idea, at a core level, that you want to feel good about yourself. Just that. Nothing else.

It is very liberating. Suddenly, all the struggles are gone. It does not mean you have or will stop caring about other things and people. It simply frees you from all your efforts and battles. It empowers you with self-acceptance, and you are free to act without reservations.

The more details, depth and thought you put into your ideas, the more valuable they become.

Simon Zingerman

You can't find the love you truly want until you live the life you truly love, because it's by living the life you love that you can model to others the love you truly want.

Lebo Grand

November 25

Relationships

Is this going anywhere? I have some important 'not being in the same room as you' to get done.

Brian Clevinger

I was very irritated because the chat we'd had about things that should be done hadn't been taken on board, I felt very disappointed, and I said so.

Whoa there.

That sounds like World War III's opening game in a little house just off the high street.

It's amazing how we try to manipulate others to do what we want. Maybe you don't, but you know people who do.

The problem with the opening statement is that it goes way back in the relationship, and when it first happened, it wasn't addressed.

If we meet someone with behaviours we dislike, we want to discuss them straight away and decide if we wish to continue the relationship. If we continue, we cannot expect them to change in five years.

If they are untidy or swear too much, when you meet them, and you continue to spend time with them, buckle up because they claimed their right to be messy and swear.

The fault is yours, not theirs.

Every day with you is an adventure I never wanted. Like swimming naked through shards of glass.

Brian Clevinger

Awareness

Do not let the roles you play in life make you forget who you are.

Roy T. Bennett

You are love.

You are peace.

You are not who you think you are.

Who you think you are is just an invention you have created to keep yourself quiet.

The truth is that at a core level, you are love, and you are peace.

We make loud noises, much banging of drums, much flashing of lights, much dashing hither and yonder to prevent us from knowing who we are.

We are stillness.

We are love.

We are peace.

We are.

Become aware. Keep returning to that awareness. Live in who you are.

Calmly accept who you are.

Adrienne Posey

November 27

Resentments

It's not worth the anger. Energy is everything. Be careful where you spend your energy – because you won't get that time back.

Tony Gaskins

Expectations are resentments in waiting or in construction.

Think about it.

You know something is going to happen.

And that it isn't quite right.

And it's their fault.

Well, that is obvious, isn't it?

Of course, it is their fault.

They don't think or care.

And so we dip our toe into resentment. Feeling hard done by. Feeling that if they cared, they'd know. They would never do that!

Now we have our foot in, no sorry, it's up to both knees, blink, and it's over your head.

And so now, wallowing in toxic resentment, we ruin the whole day, and of course, if we are clever, we can stretch it out for a week, a year, or twenty years.

I know a woman who's been married for 30 years, and hates the world because no one said she looked beautiful on her wedding day.

Get in there!

Way to go!

At the heart of all anger, all grudges, and all resentment, you'll always find a fear that hopes to stay anonymous.

Donald L. Hicks.

November 28

Happiness

Happiness cannot be travelled to, owned, earned, worn or consumed. Happiness is the spiritual experience of living every minute with love, grace and gratitude.

Denis Waitley

What would it be if I could clap my hands and make you totally happy? What would do it for you?

The trouble with that question, or the answer, is that happiness is conditional. If you think about one thing that would make you totally happy, the other things in your life would be excluded. Other things and other people.

And so, as you chase total happiness around in your head, you will realise that it is impossible because of all the missing things.

Then the conclusion has undoubtedly to be, that total happiness is impossible.

So perhaps we want to change what we are looking for. Accept and even enjoy the compromises.

Consider what we can do for others to help them be happy. And that would be nice, wouldn't it?

Happiness is not something ready-made. It comes from your own actions.

Dalai Lama

Folks are usually as happy as they make their minds up to be.

Abraham Lincoln

November 29

Gratitude

Acknowledging the good that you already have in your life is the foundation for all abundance.

Eckhart Tolle

I can NOT believe that I am writing this. (No doubt I write that sentence to delay, or perhaps even prevent my continuing to write.)

Some mornings, when I awake, I cannot go inside and find any gratitude. Why I ask myself, can I not find any gratitude? What is wrong with me? Why am I such a failure?

I can say, or think I feel grateful for... but I do not feel it.

Looking back at these times, I know my ego is jumping up and down with glee, having a field day. When I am in there, I feel such a hopeless failure.

Often, when I search for gratitude, it fills me to such an extent that I feel like a helium balloon floating up and away.

It is extraordinary, having written that, having confessed it for the first time, I realise I do not have to be perfect all the time.

I am not saying that I am perfect, I do not think that, but if I am striving for self-improvement, I hope to achieve "gratitude" a lot of the time, which is good.

No. You said I looked "okay", which is pretty much the same thing as saying, "Well, at least your nipples are covered."

Jenny Lawson

You must be okay alone with yourself before you can ever be okay with another.

Christine E. Szymanski

November 30

Insight

My father told me the story of the man who used laughing gas regularly. One day when under its influence, he claimed he knew the secret of the universe, and he managed, with immense effort, to write it down.

He got up the following day, put on his glasses and looked at the words, with fear, anticipation, and excitement, and discovered that he had written, "the smell of petroleum pervades the air." He read it again and again with disbelief, wondering if there could be some hidden meaning.

I believe that we get messages from the universe at moments in our lives. A hand that seemingly guides us to a person or a situation. And when we are lucky enough to have moments of insight, we want to grasp them fully and act on them without fear.

Nearly impossible to do, more often than not, especially as our life, routines, and our daily order is almost undoubtedly upset. So we hesitate, the moment is gone, the gate locked shut, and we travel on with our ordinary and mundane existence.

And there is nothing to be ashamed of about that. We are frail human beings. We cannot expect to be suddenly blessed with courage.

Though... perhaps next time, if we were more prepared... if we were ready... we could dare take the step that would lead us to...

Enjoying?

Share
it with
someone
else

Struggle

Together we can face any challenges as deep as the ocean and as high as the sky.

Sonia Gandhi

Oh, the challenges in life. The difficult times.

We all go through them. We all suffer.

However, we have a choice about how we react to and greet them. Often, with the cunning of denial, we pretend they are not happening until we are overwhelmed by them.

If, instead, we think of them as wonderful friends, who have come to guide us to a better life, our whole attitude toward them will change.

Nothing that happens to us needs to cause us suffering. Looking back at all that has happened in our lives, we know that we have made it through. And that will be the case now. So suffering is optional. There is always something good that comes out of everything.

I know a part of us screams, "not this time", but that is just our ego wanting to increase the suffering.

Disarm. Say thank you to the challenges and problems, and look forward to the solutions when they arrive.

The key to life is accepting challenges. Once someone stops doing this, he's dead.

Bette Davis

Don't handicap your children by making their lives easy.

Robert A. Heinlein

Wholeness

The oldest and strongest emotion of mankind is fear, and the oldest and strongest kind of fear is fear of the unknown.

H. P. Lovecraft

I am, by nature, shy. I guess I fear rejection. I fear making a fool of myself. I fear I may not say, do, or know the right thing. I fear that you will realise I am a fraud. I fear that you will think less of me. I fear that you do not want to be hugged.

Having said all that, you probably won't think of any of those things when we meet. And at some level, I know that, but that does not make it easier for me.

I have discovered that the more unconditional love I give to you, the more I receive in return. It is better to dare to risk giving myself to you and the situation.

If I view you with love, you will love me back. And that makes me feel whole.

The mind divides the world into a million pieces. The heart makes it whole.

Stephen Levine

Solutions

Only a fool thinks he can solve the world's problems.

Noah Hawley

Surely nobody would think that. That is way beyond... all hope... isn't it?

But what about my problems or your problems? That might be manageable, might it not?

Though if one thinks about it like that. Solving "ALL" my problems or "ALL" your problems. All of them?

Well, no, only a fool would think they could achieve that.

And we aren't fools, are we?

And yet we spend so much time trying to solve the unsolvable. Wrestling with this or that aspect of it. Moving this over there, pulling that over here. And in the end... well, there never is an end, is there?

Yes, we solve, change, accept one thing and replace it with another.

I'm not saying we should give up, but we can give ourselves a break.

We can change our outlook on our problems, ourselves, and others. We can think, embrace and give love to the whole shebang. And when we do, everything changes.

It is all so very much better. There is no battle.

Too often we give our children answers to remember rather than problems to solve.

Roger Lewin

December 4

Self-awareness

The worst loneliness is not to be comfortable with yourself.

Mark Twain

I remember, in my teens, times when I was in a black cloud, and everything was everybody else's fault.

Never mine.

It is so easy to snatch at the shortcomings in others and blame them for "ruining the day". Or "spoiling everything for you".

If only they had, or hadn't... then... if only...

I now know that I alone am in charge of how I feel. Of course, my ego would like to blame them, blame me, and find some clever way to criticise me and my failures.

But I have a lot of freedom from that too, because I recognise what it is doing and can (a lot of the time) discard it.

It is more enjoyable if I accept life as it unfolds and go with it without blame.

We can never obtain peace in the outer world until we make peace with ourselves.

Dalai Lama

Interaction

Yeah. I don't know, I always feel like I can't figure out how to just stop watching and actually join.

Kacen Callender

No man is an island.

John Donne

We are not meant to be islands.

We are not meant to be isolated.

When we are alone for too long, our thinking goes, and in extreme cases, we begin to go insane. Yup, totally doolally.

So, interaction with others is vital to our well-being.

But beyond that, the more we share our joys and struggles with someone else, the better it is.

Our joys are increased, filled with even greater light and delight.

While our struggles move from unscalable mountains to manageable molehills, we can accept that they will pass. That we will survive them.

For good ideas and true innovation, you need human interaction, conflict, argument, debate.

Margaret Heffernan

December 6

Respect

Respect is one of the greatest expressions of love.

Don Miguel Ruiz

Respect is so very precious and so often, and so easily overlooked.

If I respect you, I give you my time and attention when we are together. I am looking for ways that I can do things for you. I am not thinking about what I might get in return.

I have an unconditional desire to make all aspects of your life better as far as possible.

And the reward is that I then respect myself.

If I am not treating you with respect, I do not love you, and I cannot expect you to love me. You may say that you love me, but you do not love me unless you treat me with respect.

Respect yourself and others will respect you.

Confucius

I'd like to thank my mam and dad. If it wasn't for them I wouldn't have low self-esteem and have to follow this empty and shallow profession.

Johnny Vegas

December 7

Self-belief

All you need in this life is ignorance and confidence, then success is sure.

Mark Twain

In a school, they told a class that they had all been picked because they were the brightest. They told the teacher he had been selected to teach the class because he was the best.

At the end of the year, the class vastly outperformed all the other classes in the year.

And yet all the pupils and the teacher had been chosen entirely at random.

It is our self-image that determines our success.

There are so many sporting events where the underdog outplays the champion in the first half, only to be convincingly beaten in the second half by the champion. It is down to self-image and self-belief.

So it's a good idea to start increasing our self-belief and self-image in all areas of our lives. Do not contemplate failure. Do not watch or listen to negative things.

Focus on your success.

Believe. Succeed. Enjoy.

When you have confidence, you have a lot of fun. And when you have fun, you can do amazing things.

Joe Namath

December 8

Adventure

Adventure is worthwhile in itself.

Amelia Earhart

The funfair/carnival is in town.

Such happy memories of going. Different times. Different rides. Large (useless) stuffed prizes or goldfish in plastic bags. My favourite was dodgem or bumper cars.

My timid young son would only catch the yellow floating ducks to win prizes; he couldn't even be persuaded to go on the teacup ride.

I'm probably in the last quarter of my life, and I thought of going to the fair today. Alone. And then my ego screamed, "You can't do that! What will people think! They'll think you're a weirdo!"

I am so glad I don't only live with my ego. He's so f'ing tedious. Such a killjoy.

So now I'm off to the fair, on my own. Yeeha! Wahey! Hurrah!

The danger of an adventure is worth a thousand days of ease and comfort.

Paulo Coelho

Stop

Many of us have been running all our lives. Practice stopping.

Thich Nhat Hanh

Here's something you can do (or not do, really).

Can you stop doing what you're doing?

The moment you do that, something new pops into its place.

So stop doing that.

And that.

And that.

Stop doing.

Stop.

Keep peeling away until...

If you arrive (truly arrive) at nothing.

At emptiness.

Or is that wholeness?

If you arrive.

It will probably only last for a fraction of a second. But in that fraction of a second, everything changes.

Yes, everything.

I wish to tell you that it's completely okay if your life seems like a mess to you.

Rajesh Goyal

December 10

Inner Being

When we direct a lot of hostile energy toward the inner critic, we enter into a losing battle.

Sharon Salzberg

Even when we are reading, relaxing, and letting go, our ego is yakking away in the background.

Judging, poking, belittling, putting down, and even chattering on about any old rubbish that it can use to distract us.

And that's on a good day when things are going well.

God help us when things are going badly.

We can (we certainly won't if the ego can stop us) go into the peace inside us. Into the light and the calm. The ego cannot enter. We can empower ourselves, and when we return, the ego's rubbish will bounce off us like water off a windscreen.

For a while anyway.

We can do that, if we choose to.

Really, we can.

Trust your Inner-Creator and let go of your Inner-Critic.

R. J. Incer

December 11

Empathy

All I ever wanted was to reach out and touch another human being, not just with my hands but with my heart.

Tahereh Mafi

Sympathy is feeling sorry for other people's misfortune. It is detached. It does not involve us.

Empathy is the ability to understand and share the personal feelings of others.

Empathy takes effort. It means we really get in there and understand and feel what they are going through. Empathy enables us to find solutions to challenges because we are there, feeling and experiencing them.

It takes genuine involvement on our part, but the rewards that it brings make it worthwhile.

When people talk, listen completely. Most people never listen.

Ernest Hemingway

To perceive is to suffer.

Aristotle

December 12

Contact

Don't walk in front of me... I may not follow.
Don't walk behind me... I may not lead.
Walk beside me... just be my friend.

Albert Camus

Who haven't you seen or contacted for ages?
Why?
Are there people, or is there one person you feel close to, whom you have not contacted for too long?

It is a good question to consider, if not every day, at least once a week.

It is so good to get a phone call from someone who just wants to chat. It enriches both lives.

Enjoy!

We have lost contact with reality, the simplicity of life.

Paulo Coelho

December 13

Anger

Anger is a wind which blows out the lamp of the mind.

Robert Green Ingersoll

Ah anger.

Even in the most saintly of us, anger comes in and goes about its business. It's a great mistake to suppress and ignore "what they just did for the hundredth time, despite everything I've said," because then we are quietly feeding the furnace that is waiting to erupt.

We all know about the straw that broke the camel's back. "And he seemed like such a nice gentle sort of a man. I'd never have thought he'd..."

So don't store it. So don't bottle it up. Taking a long slow breath and letting it out slowly will change how you respond to it.

Also, the question, "does it really matter?" defuses it. Step sideways, let the event whizz past you, and smile as it disappears. Be calm. Be grateful that you don't have to get in there and fight. Look at the sky and be thankful you're alive. In the grand scheme of things, whatever it is will not matter in a little while, so why choose to let it matter now.

Be not angry that you cannot make others as you wish them to be, since you cannot make yourself as you wish to be.

Thomas A. Kempis

How much more grievous are the consequences of anger than the causes of it.

Marcus Aurelius

Whoa, who peed in your Cheerios?

Becca Fitzpatrick

December 14

Pain

Come mothers and fathers
Throughout the land
And don't criticise
What you can't understand.

Bob Dylan

A friend whose daughter was bullied at school yesterday has just texted me to say her daughter won't get dressed this morning.

What a milestone of emotions that creates when one hears that.

Does one bully the daughter into getting dressed?

Somehow to add bullying to bullying does not make sense.

Talk and love are surely the answer, but what energy, and commitment they take.

And what, when we, in our own way, are the bullied daughter, dragging ourselves out of bed, to return to the obnoxious.

Usually, this is what we 'have' to do, so we pull on our clothes, mentally and physically and return, eyes downcast, to the abuse, to be disrespected yet again.

Have courage.

As we know, from pain comes growth.

When we have had enough pain, we will change.

Your old roads rapidly agein'.
Please get out of the new one if you can't lend a hand
For times they are a-changin.

Bob Dylan

Behaviour

Wickedness is a myth invented by good people to account for the curious attractiveness of others.

Oscar Wilde

Sometimes, we write something as we put this book together and collectively shout, "No, we can't put that in!"

And so our dilemma. It may be too challenging, about rape, or too silly, like a limerick.

And we look and chew.

Surely we can't put that in. What will people think? They'll hate us. They'll stop reading! For example, like this one, surely we can't put this in.

And then we do.

Of course, we do.

We are human, and we love, laugh, and push each other's boundaries. We hope that you push your boundaries too. Push. Push. Go on, push some more.

The gateway to freedom is so close.

It will never open if we dare not be aggravating, funny, stupid, adventurous. Unless we dare to dare. Come in with us. The water's fine!

Don't be too timid and squeamish about your actions, all life is an experiment. The more experiments you make, the better.

Ralph Waldo Emerson

If you're offered a seat on a rocket ship, don't ask which seat, just get on.

Sheryl Sandberg

December 16

Indifference

Do I not destroy my enemies when I make them my friends.

Abraham Lincoln

Most people we feel indifferent towards do not even know that we feel this way. They are just getting on with their lives, coping as best they can with our underlying hostility.

While the people who are, or could be viewed as real enemies, are just people whose views differ from ours.

And if/when we make an effort to get to know them as human beings, the enmity between us often changes. We are far more likely to arrive at a resolution if we do that.

Fighting anyone is always counterproductive and a negative drain. We neither need nor want negative drains in our life.

At the bottom of enmity between strangers lies indifference.

Søren Kierkegaard

December 17

Blame

You only have one go at life which is thrilling. Only you can make yourself into who you want to be. Don't blame anyone else. You are entitled to free fresh air, and that is it. Do the rest yourself.

Joanna Lumley

Blaming others does not achieve anything, just hostility. We use it as a cop-out. A way to lessen our involvement. A way to feel better about ourselves. To reduce our feelings of failure.

And then there is blaming ourselves. So often, just self-flagellation so we can spiral down into the darkness of self-hatred.

Pathetic.

And, of course, walking hand in hand with blame, there is always lying.

So much better to own what we have done, accept it, and make a decision about the future.

A man can fail many times, but he isn't a failure until he begins to blame someone else.

John Bunyan

So, I went to my local supermarket and said to the guy, 'I want to make a complaint. The vinegar's got lumps in it.' He said, 'Those are pickled onions.'

Tim Vine

December 18

Patience

Have patience with all things, but first of all with yourself.

Saint Frances de Sales

Patience is a gift.

And most of all, it's a gift to ourselves. People tend to think that patience benefits others, and while it may, the person who is rewarded the most is the patient person.

Such gentle calmness when we embrace real patience. There is no stress. No negative self-harm. Just gentle peace.

We could never learn to be brave and patient, if there were only joy in the world.

Helen Keller

No wonder you're late. Why, this watch is exactly two days slow.

Lewis Carroll – Alice's Adventures in Wonderland

December 19

Self-judgement

Sometimes I just want to paint the words "It's my fault" across my forehead to save people the time of being pissed off at me.

Christina Westover

How we judge, criticise, blame, hate, and destroy ourselves is so extraordinary.

Well, no, not extraordinary we've had a lifetime of doing it in one way or another.

When a man judges himself, he finds himself guilty. (Of course, he may be guilty, but that's not the issue.)

I used to believe in heaven and hell, but now I believe that hell is what we create in ourselves and punish ourselves with. We may not do it all the time. (I hope that you're reading this thinking, "Well, this doesn't apply to me.")

However, I believe that there must have been times in your life when you crucified yourself.

Did it help? Did it improve the situation? Are you a better person because of your crucifixion? Is there anything that you can do about it now, at this moment in time?

If so, stop reading and do it.

If not, give yourself entirely to this moment. Take a deep breath. Slowly. Consciously. And as you let it out, allow your self-persecution to float away. (Continue breathing slowly until it's gone.)

If you plan to repeat whatever you feel guilty about, accept that and let go of the guilt. If you're not going to repeat it, thank yourself for letting it go.

God does not judge you, and he doesn't need to. You know how to do it to yourself.

Each person is a speck of consciousness that is attempting to awaken and return to its point of origin, to the source. That is life's true journey and story.

Belsebuub

December 20

Alone

If you're lonely when alone, you're in bad company.

Jean-Paul Sartre

Are we ever alone?

Are we not a combination of all the things we have done and all the people we've met?

And if that is the case, then surely feeling lonely is just super self-indulgence. We have such a multitude of experiences to draw upon.

The trick, if you like, is making the right choices about what we allow into our minds – now!

If we feel lonely, it is because we are enlarging negative images, filling ourselves with the pain they invoke, and then finding ways to increase the pain. At that moment, the pain is what we crave. We do our best to fill ourselves with it. We are certainly awful company.

The events and people we use to increase the pain are events and people we have also had happy times with. But we are not choosing to remember or even acknowledge the happy times. We are beating ourselves with the painful memories.

If we choose to look at, accept, or even bathe in the happy memories, the pain disappears.

We can choose to do it whenever we decide to.

Freedom is what we do with what is done to us.

Jean-Paul Sartre

December 21

Fear

A year from now you may wish you had started today.

Karen Lamb

Have you ever put off doing things?

Lack of energy, all too much effort.

Lack of appreciation, and everything or anything else conspiring to stop you.

Here's a different way to look at it, that changes perception.

What if the underlying reason for our difficulties is fear?

Fear.

We don't even need to identify the reason, cause, or type of fear. When we find ourselves thinking... I don't want to... write that report, tidy the kid's room, we can say to ourselves that's fear.

It changes the whole structure of the action we are putting off. We are now confronted with the challenge of overcoming the fear of not doing it. And often, our desire not to let fear rule us wins, and we do it with ease.

When we give ourselves compassion, we are opening our hearts in a way that can transform our lives.

Kristen Neff

December 22

Truth

Your body listens to everything you say and believes every single word. That's what one of the mentors says. Not only do your words and thoughts impact on your future, they impact on your health.

James Weeks

That bears re-reading, taking in and believing. It is awesome, profound and scary.

We want to learn to guard what we say and think. Everything that we say and think.

It affects us. It affects everyone in our lives. If we want health and happiness (presumably we do, if not, we're reading the wrong book), then that is all we want to talk about.

Never confess to illness or aches. We want to think about health, long life, and success.

If others come and dump their crap on us, we do not need to accept it. Refuse to engage in it. Focus on what you want.

The Yoruba tribe says words are like eggs. Once you drop them, things get messy.

James Weeks

Men occasionally stumble over the truth, but most of them pick themselves up and hurry off as if nothing has happened.

Winston Churchill

December 23

Death

Remember, we are not human beings having a spiritual experience. We are spiritual beings having a human experience.

Stephen Covey

I was holding my father's hand when he died. It was, he was, peaceful. I felt something leave him.

Those who report having near-death experiences, seeing the tunnel of light etc., do not talk about fear.

If we fear death, if we fear anything, it is our ego trying to maintain control of us.

Our inner being, our light, does not do fear.

Death is not to be feared. Death is just our spiritual being enjoying freedom from our body. Do not fear death.

Death may be the greatest of all human blessings.

Socrates

December 24

Journeys

*Never be in a hurry; do everything quietly and in a calm
spirit. Do not lose your inner peace for anything
whatsoever, even if your whole world seems upset.*

Saint Francis De Sales

Our life is a journey. What is important about a journey is
what is happening now, not the destination.

It's mapped out, and we have places to go, things to see
and learn. And if we don't see or understand them the first
time around, don't worry. They will come around again.

So really, there is no need to do fear. What is coming will
come, and it will pass. Knowing that we can choose to feel
peace, however hard the current struggle may be. It will
pass. So choose peace now.

A quiet mind cureth all.

Robert Burton

December 25

Giving

It's not how much we give, but how much love we put into giving.

Mother Teresa

Today is a day for giving.
Today is a day to make the world a better place.
A better place for the world and a better place for you.
Whenever you can, wherever you are, whoever you are with, give compliments and encourage people. Everyone. Oh, if you can't manage everyone, then most people.
Enjoy the experience as the magic spreads.

No one is useless in this world who lightens the burdens of another.

Charles Dickens

You cannot find peace by avoiding life.

Virginia Woolf

December 26

Self-image

The only thing that matters in life, is your own opinion about yourself.

Osho

Self-image is amazing.

I am dyslexic, and when I went to school a long time ago, they didn't know about it. I was labelled thick or stupid, and although I have overcome dyslexia and have had a successful life, there is still somewhere in the back of my mind the notion that I am not clever enough.

And not just clever enough, I feel that I am a failure. That I am less than. That you look down on me.

I know it isn't true, and I can discard the thought when it pops into my mind. But it is there.

To some extent, we all have an incorrect self-image that will damage us when it can, if we allow it to.

A poor self-image is the magnifying glass that can transform a trivial mistake or an imperfection into an overwhelming symbol of personal defeat.

David D. Burns

December 27

Stillness

Anything you want to ask a teacher, ask yourself and wait for the answer in silence.

Byron Katie

We know so so much more than we imagine.

The trouble is the noise being constantly shouted by our ego in an attempt to keep us ignorant.

"Attempts" does not do it justice, "success" is much closer to the mark. It constantly keeps us locked in a room of distraction.

And most people go to their grave, never having silenced it. We do not have to be one of them. We know how to go inside. We know how to be still. We know how to stop and listen. We know where peace and joy are.

Stillness is where creativity and solutions to problems are found.

Eckhart Tolle

Living

When we give ourselves compassion, we are opening our hearts in a way that can transform our lives.

Kristin Neff

We know, by now, that the ego, loud, brash child that it is, wants our total attention. It wants to rule and manipulate us into doing what it wants. And it achieves that by controlling us with anxiety and fear, making us long to have and do things that perpetuate its god-like existence in our lives.

It wants us to be angry, to feel "right" more right than anyone else and to fear that we are wrong, more wrong than everyone else.

And yet we know by now, that we have another voice, another way to be, another way we can choose.

Call it your inner voice, your higher power/self, your soul. Call it what you will, it exists. It waits there, waiting for us to choose it. It is forgiveness, love and peace.

We got our training as children from people who worshipped and lived within the grasp of the ego, so naturally, that is how we think we should behave. And to stop behaving like that probably seems totally irresponsible.

However, we know how wonderful it is to have peace. And that comes to us when we choose the other way to live, and share forgiveness and love wherever we are.

Those who flow as the life flows know they need no other force.

Lao Tzu

December 29

Judgement

To speak ill of others is a dishonest way of praising ourselves.

Will Durant

So very easy to do.

And not just the big complaints or judgements we may make, but also the little, almost habitual ones.

They all imply, "I don't do that", or even " I am so much better than them because I would never even dream of doing that".

And I know that I still do this, though far less often than I used to.

I am, after all, a work in progress.

Enjoy guarding against it.

The trouble with most people is that they think with their hopes or fears or wishes rather than with their minds.

Will Durant

Emotions

Time doesn't heal emotional pain. You need to learn how to let go.

Roy T. Bennett

Let your emotions out. Let out your pain as well as your love. Do not deny them and push them down where they can fester and poison you.

I'm not talking about the attack emotions of anger, jealousy, envy and sulking. They are thoughts and reactions which we choose to have. We can choose not to have them.

For example, we can choose not to do anger. If we do anger, the person we are hurting is ourselves. We can choose peace rather than anger.

But real emotions like grief we want to express and let out so that we can move on from them. If we pretend that we are not suffering, we store the suffering inside. Waiting there to smash us later.

And love. We want to express our love as fully as we can. For with the joy of love, there is also, in waiting, the pain that comes when it changes.

We want the intensity of love to last forever. But it doesn't. And we want to learn to accept and release the pain that comes when it changes. Then we can be whole and continue to love, accepting its new form with love.

Sometimes the hardest part isn't letting go but rather learning to start over.

Nicole Sobon

December 31

Thinking

How twisted our thinking becomes when we are afraid.

Karen Casey

When we are afraid, we are in the hands of our ego, which continues to drag us down in whatever way it can. That is how it controls us.

We have the other voice inside us, the still and quiet voice of love, peace and serenity.

If we stop long enough to listen, to find it. It is there. Peace and calm are there.

We want to ask ourselves, which voice do I want to listen to? Which voice makes life possible and worth embracing?

At first, we may have to constantly stop, ask ourselves, and remake our choice. But the more often we do it, the easier and the more automatic it becomes. Peace of mind is possible.

The primary cause of unhappiness is never the situation, but your thoughts about it. Be aware of the thoughts you are thinking.

Eckhart Tolle

Freedom	Jan 23	Feb 5	May 7	May 24
	Aug 24	Sept 11	Nov 12	
Giving	Mar 30	Dec 25		
Goals	May 11			
God	May 21			
God's Children	Aug 29			
Gold	Jan 30			
Gratitude	Feb 24	Oct 18	Nov 29	
Growing up	Sept 28			
Guiding	July 25			
Habit	Nov 19			
Handing Over	May 19	June 5		
Happiness	Jan 17	Mar 28	Nov 28	
Harvesting	Mar 6	Oct 19		
Heart	Nov 6			
Hell	Jan 31			
Help	May 13			
Honesty	May 23			
Hugging	July 6			
Illness	Oct 25			
Inactivity	Mar 7			
Indifference	Aug 10	Dec 16		
Inner Being	July 3	Aug 7	Dec 10	
Insecurity	Nov 7			
Insight	Nov 30			
Intention	Feb 2			
Interaction	Feb 8	Dec 5		
Intimacy	Sept 14			
Involvement	Feb 10			
Journeys	Dec 24			
Joy	Oct 27			
Judgement	Jan 5	Feb 22	June 4	Oct 22
	Dec 29			
Laughter	Feb 19	Mar 18		
Leaf	Jun 22			

Printed in Great Britain
by Amazon